The Executive's Illustrated Primer Of Long-Range Planning

The Executive's Illustrated Primer Of Long-Range Planning

DICK LEVIN
School of
Business Administration
University of North Carolina

*(With lots of help from
Ginger Travis and John Branch)*

Library of Congress Cataloging in Publication Data

LEVIN, RICHARD I (date)
   The executive's illustrated primer of long-range planning.

   Includes bibliographical references and index.
   1. Corporate planning. I. Title.
HD30.28.L48   658.4′012   80-14955
ISBN 0-13-294140-6

Editorial/production supervision and interior
   design by Richard C. Laveglia
Page layout by Anne Bonanno
Illustrated by John Branch
Cover design by Edsal Enterprises
Manufacturing buyer: Gordon Osbourne

Printed in the United States of America
10   9   8   7   6   5   4   3   2   1

Prentice-Hall International, Inc., *London*
Prentice-Hall of Australia Pty. Limited, *Sydney*
Prentice-Hall of Canada, Ltd., *Toronto*
Prentice-Hall of India Private Limited, *New Delhi*
Prentice-Hall of Japan, Inc., *Tokyo*
Prentice-Hall of Southeast Asia Pte. Ltd., *Singapore*
Whitehall Books Limited, *Wellington, New Zealand*

For Debbie, Steve, and Lisa . . .
the real writers in the family

CONTENTS

PREFACE

When I decided to write a long-range planning book I had four goals: First, it had to be *practical*. I guess I've read about as much of the literature on long-range planning as most folks, and I find textbook approaches to the subject of little value for practicing managers. So here you'll find very direct language and lots of examples. Planning is still an art, not a science, and my examples are here to show how the art can be tailored to specific situations (with a little luck, of course). Second, it had to be *illuminating* . . . vivid enough to answer most of the questions practicing managers have about long-range planning, (things like why do we need it, how should we start, what is long range, who should do it), and with a particular focus on the manager's problems in trying to make it work (or diagnosing why it didn't). Third, it needed to be *honest*. Accordingly, you'll find a number of instances where I just plain don't know and say so, or personal examples where I didn't know, tried anyhow, and managed to screw it up royally. I don't mind both of us laughing at me together. And finally, it had to be *fun*, fun to write and fun to read, thus the anecdotal style. But hidden under the anecdotes is my twenty-five years of long-range planning, (the successes *and* the failures). I hope you find this distillation of my experience useful in making long-range planning work in your career.

Dick Levin
Chapel Hill, N. C.

ONE

Introduction and Chapter Preview

What kind of nut would spend
all this time writing when the
fish are biting so good?

*Schemes lightly made come to nothing,
but with long planning they succeed.*

Proverbs

At last count there were just short of 500 published articles and 79 books on the subject of long-range planning, bearing out the sage of *Ecclesiastes* who said, "Of making many books there is no end, and much study is weariness of the flesh." I agree with the sage, hence this promise: this book will be short, practical, true to the real world—and it will not weary your flesh. I wrote it with George Allen, late of the Washington Redskins, in mind.

George Allen is a personal hero of mine even though he doesn't know me from a goalpost. From 1971 through 1977, George's over-the-hill gang, a.k.a. the Redskins, transformed my Sundays. His contrary wisdom in trading his first-, third-, fourth-, and eighth-round draft picks for Billy Kilmer and assorted superannuated Rams that first year made me a genius in hindsight two years later. When winning through geriatric intimidation became his trademark, I considered dying my hair gray to show my devotion. By the end of the glory that was the 1972 season, my hero had proved himself a turnaround artist extraordinaire at Washington, and I suddenly knew that I could be one too—if there was just an NFL franchise I could afford. I identified.

There is only one point on which we ever disagreed. His critics used to say, "George, you're mortgaging your future for the present. This trading youth for age is like living on your capital. It has to stop." I paid no attention, blinded by loyalty. The day the scales fell from my eyes was the day George Allen said, "Hell, the only future I'm interested in is this Sunday afternoon."

I'm here to tell you, George, that as surely as the sun will rise, Monday morning comes. And beyond Monday, next year, next season. I believe that even in pro football and politics there is a long term beyond the next game, the next election. I think that you are one hell of a strategist, George Allen, but your time horizon is too short. Out of my admiration and my debt for those good Sundays, this book, George Allen—everything I know and can tell about planning for the other side of Sunday—is for you.

This short book is written, too, for anyone who holds responsibility for the long-term success of an organization, who has to answer the question, "What next, coach?" It is for men and women in public and private endeavors who plan for the future—or who think perhaps that they should and aren't sure, or know that they should but don't know why, or know why but not how or how but not why. It is not a scholarly book, even though I am a teacher. (If you need a scholarly work, there are those 500 published articles and 79 books, which ought to fill the bill.) I will from time to time, however, borrow ideas from a couple of pragmatic scholars whose thoughts I've admired and used with success for many years. Although facets of long-range planning have lately become painfully technical, not to say arcane, I will stick with simple ideas and workable suggestions on a nontechnical level. Finally, I'll illustrate ideas and suggestions with examples of what my friends and associates have tried, for better or worse, along with a few playbacks of my own experiences in planning. You'll meet roughly a hundred men and women who run organizations that I've worked for or with during the past 25 years. From their planning triumphs, disasters, or failures to plan at all, from their good common sense and willingness to grapple with uncertainty, we should arrive at the reasons why organized activities need long-range planning, what long-range planning really is, how it works, how you do it successfully, and some things to avoid when you try it.

ANSWERING OBJECTIONS

Of course, some people think it's bunk.

1. "It's hard work that made this business what it is today, not pie-in-the-sky stuff."

Interpretation: Virtue looketh not beyond the end of its nose.

2. "It's no use. You make a long-range plan and the Feds are there in six months telling you it's illegal. If you're in compliance, they change the law."

Interpretation: I am so persecuted. Boy, wouldn't I secretly like to be a Fed kicking ass all day.

3. "You can't plan. Look at Pearl Harbor. Look at the Galveston Tidal Wave and the Johnstown Flood. Look at OPEC. Look at Elvis Presley. I mean, you just don't know when these things will happen."

Interpretation: Let's face it, planning is hard work and I prefer tennis. I take the stance "a bolt from the blue can strike anywhere"; it gives me more time to practice.

4. "I started injection molding subwidgies in my garage in 1958 with my own process. I survived the shakeout of '69. I cashed out last year for $20 million, the biggest subwidgie supplier east of the Mississippi. You think I did that drawing decision trees with 49 branches?"

Interpretation: I'm an untutored genius, kid, and I'm tough. You look a little effete to me. Sure you haven't got one of those MBA degrees or anything like that?

Given that bad news makes news, an appeal to the past offers little encouragement. History is replete with disaster and chagrin. It affords plenty of ammunition to pessimists in its record of untimely random occurrences and ill-starred coincidences.

Consider Napoleon's hemorrhoids at Waterloo. If Napoleon had only known Murphy of Murphy's law (if something can go wrong, it will), they might be speaking French in Austria, Germany, and Russia today. But who could have predicted that Napoleon's hemorrhoids would have chosen that historic moment to act up? But for a trivial medical episode and its reputed impact on his thinking that day, Napoleon might have had the good sense to head off Field Marshall Blucher's forces at the pass, so to speak, and thus have prevented them from joining forces with the Allied armies under the Duke of Wellington. Imagine the headlines in the Paris newspapers if that had happened: June 18, 1815, "Napoleon Defeats Wellington at Waterloo. Entire Course of 19th Century European History to Change."

Consider Alexander the Great, the most successful 33-year-old in some time, extraordinary strategist, conqueror of the eastern Mediterranean, Egypt, and the Persian Empire, on the eve of an Arabian campaign, who sat down in 323 B.C. to a ten-day bout of eating and drinking and never got up again. He planned ultimately to conquer India. He had survived the fevers, wounds, and deprivations of soldiering since the age of 16. All this to die by surprise of a gastric indiscretion in Asia? It doesn't do much for those who carry the banner, "Planning Pays Off."

Or consider the cranberry growers of 1959, whose more modest goal than conquest was just to have a bumper year (a goal well founded upon the Department of Agriculture forecast for the 1959 harvest). Imagine their making the final projections of Thanksgiving and Christmas sales volumes, the meticulously ciphered pro formas of the more affluent growers pointing up the value of "knowing exactly where we're going." That is, just before Secretary Flemming of HEW announced that cranberries sprayed with the weed killer aminotriazole might cause cancer—two weeks before Thanksgiving. The rest is history (a footnote to which was Mrs. Flemming's serving the Secretary cranberries on Thanksgiving Day to show confidence in clean berries—remember that? Of course not. The bias of history is to pessimism.) Anyhow, no one can possibly blame the National Cranberry Institute for failing in its wildest conjecture to see that crusher coming.

Enough of gloom and doubt. If we learn anything from history, it is that our future will be full of good and bad surprises: Soviet missiles in Cuba, Sadat's peace initiative to Israel, the sudden American thaw toward China, the OPEC price hikes. But complaining that life is uncertain is like complaining that kissing may give you "mono" (or something worse). It may. But would you quit?

IT ISN'T JUST ROULETTE, MA

Only a fool overlooks the impact of chance, of sudden initiative, of accident or stupidity. But, by the same token, only the same fool bets his or her organization's future on the premise that the entire environment of public and private enterprise is completely capricious and random. Long-range planners who've been at it for a while recognize that unplanned events will always occur despite good plans, that they will do so at the most embarrassing and inopportune times (Levin's Corollary to Murphy's law), and that there is little or no formal administrative defense to prevent all such disruptions. Having taken that position, however, the good planners I know size up their environment as being more ordered than random, more structured than disarrayed, more benign than malevolent, more knowable than inscrutable—thus more likely to respond positively and profitably to intelligent, consistent, well-planned strategies than to shots in the dark. (Nor are these brave souls deterred by the risks from kissing, breathing, or crossing the street.)

If the occasional craps that environments roll in the face of good long-range plans damage you psychologically, being a long-range planner is number 11 on a list of 9 professional undertakings that you should consider. If, on the other hand, you survive the occasional strike, fire, financial panic, inventory shortage, or political skirmish without hitting the Maalox, read on. We just may have something here you'll like.

EARLY PEACHES TEACH HUMILITY

When I was 18 and had just finished my freshman year in engineering, my father (a very wise, poker-playing, smooth-talking produce broker) sent me to Inman, South Carolina to open up a peach-packing plant. All he really expected me to do was oil the motors, align the belts, and sweep up—tasks he felt suited an engineer. Undaunted, and supported by hundreds of precise (but hardly accurate) calculations made on my K and E Log-Log Decitrig Duplex slide rule, I singlehandedly, and completely without authorization, bested a dumb old farmer by the masterful purchase of his entire crop of early peaches for an incredibly low price. When my father called me to check on the motors and belts (and the sweeping), I generously offered to cut him in on half the profits, estimated by me then at something over $3,000.

"No," he said, "you did all the work, you should get all the profits." "My God," I thought, "a truly generous man." Two weeks later, by sheer dint of my father's connections in the produce market, along with the generosity of our New York broker, they managed to hold "my" losses on that crop to $900. My father, a good poker player, said nothing. When the season ended two months later and I was heading back to engineering school for more wisdom, he handed me a check for $300 for 12 weeks' work. For a split second there, I almost reminded him that our original deal had been $100 a week. But even engineers finally learn to cipher human equations.

Since that summer, I have made and lost enough money, won and folded enough poker hands, and hit and missed on enough opportunities to bring some humility as well as experience to the writing of this book. I like what Adlai Stevenson said about experience best:

> What a man knows at 50 that he did not know at 20 boils down to something like this: The knowledge he has acquired with age is not a knowledge of formulas, of forms, of words, but of people, places, actions—as knowledge not gained by words but by touch, sight, sound; victories, failures, sleeplessness, devotion, love—the human experience and emotions of this earth and of one's self and other men. Perhaps, too, a little faith, a little reverence for things you cannot see.[1]

In long range-planning, what turns input into insight is creativity, experience, long thought. Although planners are technically supported by experts with computer modeling, sampling techniques, and statistical packages, planning is art. So I would underscore Stevenson's "a little faith, a little reverence for things you cannot see." Planners need a touch of optimism to live with the inevitability of change, especially change in forms that they know cannot be foreseen.

COMING ATTRACTIONS

I had a marvelous economics professor in graduate school, Clarence Philbrook, who used to say, "If you don't understand the *philosophy* of economics, you'll never master the dismal science." Chapter 2 is my philosophical pitch for long-range planning. I know too many executives who simply don't know what planning is, why organizations need to do it, and what it can accomplish. Interestingly, however, most of them think they do and are persuaded their planning is first class. They're like people who believe that you attend cocktail parties to drink, go bass fishing for food, or fly your own plane for transportation. They miss the critical essence of the activity. So before we get involved in How, we need to master Why. That's Chapter 2.

Chapter 3 is how to do it, step by step: what you do first, second, third; how you start, how you proceed, how you finish, and when to quit if you don't quite finish. Philosophically, there should be no difference between the long-range planning process of large and small organizations. Pragmatically, however, this chapter approaches How To Do It from two different size perspectives. First, we look at the larger, more formal, and complex organization with personnel who specialize in the planning area. Second, we do it for the smaller, more entrepreneurial, one-person type of show where the line between planners and doers really doesn't exist and where they can't afford the Chase Econometric Forecast (at least not regularly).

Chapter 4 raises the most commonly asked operational questions and even takes a shot at answering them: How many years into the future do you plan for? Who should do planning in the organization? Should planning be centralized or decentralized? How do you know when your plan is right for you? Should you plan from the outside in or from the inside out? What's the difference between extrapolative planning and entrepreneurial planning and when should you use each? In every instance, we'll avoid doctrinaire views (my worst doctrinaire view at 18 was that slide rules were for solving important problems). Instead, we'll concentrate on answers that can work for many different organizations facing a wide array of problems in different planning environments.

So you've got a plan—now can you get the troops to follow? Read Chapter 5, Behavioral Considerations. What's the role of the leader in long-range planning, how do you get participation in and commitment to planning goals, how do you plan and conduct a successful long-range planning "retreat"? We'll consider the relationship between the leader's management style and the kind of planning goals that tend to be set as a result of that style. We'll consider how not to get trapped by measuring inputs instead of outputs in planning, how you know when your people are taking appropriate risks as opposed to excessive or insufficient ones, planning horizons in relation to a key individual's remaining tenure in the organization, all issues that become germane when you attempt to "lay off" your plan on the rest of the organization. How to get the gang to go along with you—I'll show you some examples of how successful executives have done it and how they occasionally botched the job—a few private solutions to nagging behavioral constraints.

Chapter 6 is for special planning environments. These are situations that generously reward a more finely tuned and specific approach. For example, planning for new ventures will be examined, along with planning for government agencies, doomsday plans, contingency planning, "end of game" plans, planning procedures for "follower" companies and "leader" companies, planning approaches when this is the first plan, and a workable approach to starting over when the last plan was a disaster.

Chapter 7 shows that all good long-range plans are based both on assumptions about the way that things are likely to be out to the planning horizon—estimation—and the way that they have been in the past—extrapolation. An incredible number of people in this world do nothing but research and compile data about the way the world was, is, and likely will be. The problem has always been for people to locate data sources pertinent to their specific industry, location, time horizon, or market situation without spending an inordinate amount of time or money doing so. This is particularly true of organizations with no planning data expert, those in which doers must take time off to put on their planning hat. Chapter 7 is a comprehensive listing of almost all the standard data sources useful for long-range planning and available at this time. This chapter has been included to shed light on such questions as "Charlie, where do I find the number of cars that were imported from Belgium last year?" (Actually, the answer is zero.) Or "Louise, can you get me three good estimates of disposable income for New Jersey for the next five years?" Chapter 7 contains 88 individual citations of private and public data sources for long-range planning, some free, some quite expensive, but each of possible use to an organization in a specific planning situation. This chapter is included to let you see what's available and how to get it without wasting time wondering or searching.

EARLY PEACHES: REPRISE
AND A CONCLUSION

Back to Inman, South Carolina and the early peach crop for a parting thought. After that debacle, I experienced the revelations of hindsight and told my father what I'd do right if I could just do it over. "And if a toad had wings," he replied, "he wouldn't beat his ass to death on the ground." So here you are: a well-made plan is a set of wings. It will not always work perfectly, and sometimes you'll land in the mud through circumstances beyond the control of your most elegant strategy. But, believe me, planning and flying sure beats pounding your ass to death on the ground.

Up, up, and away.

NOTES

[1] From an address by Adlai E. Stevenson at Princeton University, March 23, 1954, reported in the *New York Herald Tribune,* March 23, 1954.

TWO

Developing a Long-Range Planning Mindset

Just when you think you know
what it is that you're supposed
to be doing, you find out
you ain't.

I am the master of my fate,
I am the captain of my soul.

W. E. Henley

Not without a plan, you're not.

R. I. Levin

Long-range planning reminds me of bird hunting. Shotgun in hand, approaching the field, you're sure that somewhere in the stubble there are birds (the objective). Might be just under your feet or half a mile away. Sometimes they freeze right beside your feet, invisible. Other times, just for meanness, they fly out the other end of the field whistling, "Eat your heart out, bird hunter, you were never even close." Suppose that you get lucky, you stumble on the birds, the covey explodes under your feet—by the time you've fumbled the safety off your Browning, those birds are halfway to the county line still gaining speed. Talk about frustrated: you turn into the risk-taking hunter, walking with a gun held ready in front, safety off. You step high to avoid tripping, your back and shoulders aching to divorce your body. Suddenly an unexpected rising of quail under your feet—you'd just stopped believing in their existence—a jerk in your finger, a bang, and one of two outcomes: (1) you just shot your toes off in fright; (2) you just shot your brother-in-law next to you. In either event, the objective was not realized.

Examining this situation carefully, we find that, of all the factors in successful bird hunting, the only one not under the hunter's control is timing—specifically, having enough time to react effectively: ready, aim, fire, retrieve dead bird. Recognizing a bird is not at issue; aiming and firing are learnable skills. But, in the final analysis, it's not having enough time to react sensibly that compels the bird hunter to resort to his own long-range planning system, the dog!

Enter bird dog. The dog can't aim a gun, doesn't know a good bird hunting day from a bad one, doesn't really like to eat birds, can't cook one, and had rather stay home chasing fleas and napping. What does the dog really do? The dog is the long-range plan in the bird-hunting system. It works like this. Dog ranges far and wide over the field twice as fast as a man can walk, its uncanny nose held low, working that cover for birds. Sensing birds near, it slows, stops, freezes on a point, and holds it while the hunter does his or her best to catch up before Christmas is over. The birds hold, the dog holds, the hunter takes position, clicks the safety off, glances around his or her field of fire to make sure that brother-in-law is out of the way. Now the strategy in action: hunter signals dog to get up the birds, the dog galvanizes into action, and the covey explodes all around the hunter, who, being prepared, picks a target, fires, picks another, fires, and winds up two for two with his or her double-barreled Browning. That's what timing can do for you.

HUNTING FOR DOUBLE-KNITS

There is, of course, a parallel to organizational behavior and decisions. Some years ago when double-knit fabrics were first coming into fashion, a large Southern textile firm was hunting without a bird dog; it was two years before management recognized that the field was full of birds. Being men of consequential technical abilities, they geared up to produce double-knits with a vengeance—much like rolling cannon up to a field just as the birds begin to leave. Several years later when double-knits went out of fashion, they still hadn't bought a dog, and the knitting machines went clacking on two years too long. Needless to say, they lost their fondness for bird hunting on that deal.

Moral: Bird hunting and chasing fashion has this to tell us. The *raison d'etre* of long-range planning is to create a condition in which top management of the organization takes an active role rather than a passive one; that is, the top executives retain the strategic development prerogative *within* the organization rather than let it get away to the outside, where it can only serve the best interests of others. Another way of saying it: the purpose of long-range planning is to keep management the master of the organization's fate. Otherwise, competitors, unions, regulatory agencies, special interest groups, even impersonal social and economic trends will settle the hash of any organization that defaults in the planning function.

In bird-hunting terms, management wants to bag the most birds that it can and avoid getting shot by other hunters. Smart management buys the best bird dog it can find for the money. The managerial equivalent of that bird dog is strategic planning.

SUNDAYS AND STRATEGY

The process of determining a uniquely appropriate strategy for an organization is referred to as strategic long-range planning. Recall George Allen's strategy of building a winning team immediately by trading draft picks for veteran players ("the only future . . . is this Sunday afternoon"). As in elective politics, the underlying assumption is win for the fans this Sunday and the future will take care of itself; that is, management will renew your contract, and somehow replacements will be found for those aging receivers, but not to worry until then. Contrast the Dallas Cowboys under Tom Landry, whose strategy has been to scout new talent at the college level, draft players, condition them rigorously, bring them up through the Dallas system, and keep them at Dallas. Landry's strategy took longer, but he built a team that could go the distance year after year. The result, as one fan put it, turned out to be the IBM of professional football. Landry and Allen chose diametrically opposed strategies for building a winning football team, but each strategy worked for the particular coach and his organization, out to the coach's time horizon.

The objective in strategy formulation is to determine for the organization (or individual) a specific course of action uniquely appropriate to:

1. the opportunities available in the environment
2. the risks associated with those opportunities

3. the resources available to the organization
4. the personal values of the organization's leadership as well as constituency—in particular their preference for risk taking

Strategic planning begins by defining what business the organization *is* in and what business it *should be* in, giving consideration to all four factors just cited. (It is perfectly legitimate to keep on doing what you're already doing if that looks like a winner out to your time horizon.) The beginning point, once more, in strategic planning is to take a hard look at the organization, the environment, the opportunities, and the risks.

Returning to the career of Alexander the Great before his demise from overindulgence as noted in the previous chapter, we can take a lesson from a brilliant and flexible strategist in the art of tailoring the plan to fit leadership ability, military resources, and risk preference. When Alexander became commander of the Macedonian army at the age of 20, his goal was to conquer the Persian Empire of Darius. His first task was to remove the Persian navy from the eastern Mediterranean; otherwise Greece would be exposed to counterattack as Alexander marched into Asia. Because he was not a naval commander, Alexander devised the simple strategy, as he put it, "to defeat the Persian fleet on land." With his army, he proceeded to conquer the coast of the entire eastern Mediterranean from modern Turkey south through Syria, Lebanon, and Israel, to Egypt. It took Alexander three years from crossing the Dardanelles into Asia to finish the conquest of Egypt. But the success of his strategy was complete; his Greek army defeated the Persian navy on land by taking away every port. He then, at the age of 25, turned east to pursue Darius into the heart of the Persian Empire.

It is essential that strategy be uniquely determined for each separate organization at each separate time in its history. Although it is often tempting to export standard strategy in place of uniquely formulated strategy, the subtle differences in the environment and in the organization only rarely tolerate this approach. Winston Churchill said it well:

> In the problems which the Almighty sets his humble servants, things hardly ever happen the same way twice over, or if they seem to do so, there is some variant which stultifies undue generalization.[1]

The technology of warfare had changed so much between the two world wars as to make most military strategy nonexportable from the 1914–1918 conflict to the 1939–1945 conflict, even though the same combatants returned to the same battleground. The Maginot Line offers a classic example of the failure of strategy that became outdated. Before World War II the French had built a system of fixed defensive outposts with strongly fortified pillboxes to guard the eastern frontier. In essence it was a stationary line of defense designed for the style of fighting in World War I. But, instead of hundreds of thousands of troops in trenches battling for a few yards of ground, the German armored divisions set the fighting style of World War II: fewer men moving faster, mobility and deployed firepower rendering useless a fixed line of defense.

In business, what's left of A & P is a grim reminder that a strategy that earned half a billion dollars for 50 years had a very definite life span. (Texaco knew the value of a *uniquely determined strategy* at least in their advertising; they used to advertise, with outstanding results, that their gasoline was "locally blended" for your individual needs—and all this time I thought it came out of the same pipeline.)

Not long ago a very successful hamburger chain in North Carolina almost bought the farm when it ventured into the shrimp business with no changes from its beef operation. But how you buy shrimp is not how you buy beef, and how you sell it isn't the same. Cloning the hamburger strategy did not produce a clone; it produced a balance sheet mutant.

All strategies are time-relevant. Organizations that forget this maxim by and large drive good horses right into the ground. Long-range planning is based on the premise that change is the order of the day, that it is both a ubiquitous and inevitable part of the environment, and, therefore, that the same strategy cannot succeed forever with the same degree of success.

Bird hunters, take note: strategies and hunting dogs wear out. Buy or breed new ones, and use the right dog. Gunning for quail, take a pointer; when it's ducks, a retriever.

SOMETIMES YOU DON'T THINK
UP THE WHOLE THING
WEDNESDAY MORNING

Although a finished strategy may be simply stated (especially in retrospect and especially when proved successful), formulating the strategy is not always quick or simple. A persistent myth has the entire board of directors of IBM deciding in a three-hour meeting the ten-year future course of the corporation. What a myth. James Brian Quinn of Dartmouth University points out that, although IBM's System 360 single-product strategy probably was conceived as early as 1959 when management noticed that the division's products had begun to overlap, it was not until well into the 1970s that the System 360 strategy dissipated as the essential strength of the corporation. During this 15-year period of developing and implementing one strategy, the plan underwent many alterations and refinements. Nonetheless, it still took 15 years for IBM to conceive, develop, implement, and exploit a single strategy.

What looks simple in retrospect, a good workable strategy, can be complex in the making because, as Quinn points out, in the beginning there may be too many unknowns to formulate a complete strategy in one stroke. Technical problems, financial uncertainties, marketing decisions, organizational needs, psychological commitments, resource bases, and political support all take time to solve or build, precluding successful "instant strategy." ("Add product and stir. Increase market share 20 percent in one year's time.") Strategy formulation *is* often complex in real life. The process may be

19

difficult and take a long time. But one thing it is not: strategy formulation is *not* a random process. Beneath the details particular to a specific place and time and group of people, a general pattern emerges of the strategy-making process:[2]

1. *Sensing needs:* Executives sense a need—often in a very vague, general way—that a strategic change is needed for the organization.

2. *Building awareness:* Not everyone senses the same need, so it is essential to build a wider awareness through the organization of this sensed need. Consciously or unconsciously, at this point the politics of gaining acceptance for a good idea has begun. The game is to get the key organizational players comfortable enough with the new idea to take risk on its behalf—you could call this building a comfort factor.

3. *Crystallizing the developing focus:* The shrewd top executive—even one committed to a Theory Y management style—recognizes the importance of closure. Thus by judicious

choice of committee membership, task force make-up, and personnel appointments, he or she influences the direction strategy is taking and often adds to the speed with which closure is reached.

4. *Generating real commitment:* The experienced executive gets commitment by making single individuals accountable for specific goals. Here the executive is looking for that zeal, effort, and energy that come only when an individual identifies with the goal and knows that his or her future is tied to it. Psychologists call this "ownership." It works.

Quinn has labeled this approach to strategic long-range planning "logical incrementalism." In life it works out to be the delicate art of step-by-step goal setting through vision, entrepreneurship, and politics. Effective top executives tend to avoid simplistic, formal planning gimmicks, Theory Y management, achievement management style, MBO-type approaches, or any single way that promises to do it all. Effective top executives usually work through a consensus-building approach—in essence, through politics. (The checklist approach does not exist in political life.) Franklin D. Roosevelt aroused animosity and controversy with his politics. Yet he inspired a consensus among such disparate groups as labor, blacks, and liberals—previously fragmented—to create the powerful Democratic coalition.

BUT WHAT WILL THEY SAY
BACK IN HIGH POINT?

Though most of us don't operate in spheres, as does IBM, that permit or reward strategy development over a 15-year period, we need to recognize that the process of generating "ownership" is pretty much the same everywhere. I have a friend who owns a small furniture plant. He and I used to spend a couple of days a year thinking about what the company ought to be when it grew up. Every time we came to a strategic turning point that I felt merited agreement on his part, he'd say, "Let me go home, Dick, and let the boys chew on that one awhile." Make no mistake, he was a sure enough hard-ass manager, but a clever politician too. He understood quite well what "ownership" meant. The boys back in High Point had to buy the plan.

Although strategic long-range planning always considers changes in strategy, it may legitimately reaffirm the appropriateness of the current strategy (to the chagrin of those professional planners who in their zeal equate any change with progress, not to mention the justification of their own jobs). The final recommendation of a long-range plan may be not to change a winning act. If so, stand pat. But make sure beforehand that you've got good intelligence that the environment will not change soon or suddenly. Or you could consider putting a half nelson on the change agents as another way of assuring stability. Sixty years ago, for instance, if you'd wanted to stay in the electric trolley business, you'd have been damn smart to cut Henry Ford in on the deal. (But you didn't, so it must be your fault that I have to drive all the way to San Francisco to ride a trolley anymore.)

Moral: Intelligence gathering followed by careful analysis of opportunities, risks, and trends in the environment is the foundation upon which strategic planning is built. Going through the process keeps the organization alert even when the outcome is no change for now. (If your product is Lifesavers, Hershey bars, or Ivory soap, don't fiddle with the formula. Do glance around periodically; if you don't spot any alligators, you can still enjoy the view.)

RIDING THE RANGE
WITH MY DOGIES AND
MY LONG-RANGE PLAN

Thus far we've looked at strategic planning as a conscious function, particularly in large organizations where whole staffs devote themselves to planning activity. Smaller organizations are usually different. Entrepreneurs are the romantics of business and industry, the risk takers out riding a personal range, impatient of fences. Think they'd own up to a four-dollar phrase like strategic long-range planning?

My wife's cousin Mike is a knock-off artist in New York. He sees a dress style in from Paris on Tuesday, he has a contract pattern maker make patterns by Friday, he has a contract cutter cut 250 dresses by the next Tuesday, and his contract sewer has the finished dresses in Mike's shipping room ten days later. In a little less than three weeks, Mike has 250 finished dresses in his customers' stores. Mike has four full-time employees including himself, and he'll do over $2 million worth of business this year on zero fixed assets (he even leases his desk and car) and on nearly zero current assets (he factors virtually all his inventories and receivables). The last time that he was in Chapel Hill, Mike came along to one of my MBA classes for a free show. Afterward he laughed at the seriousness of my students (he always laughs at me) in their devotion to strategy. "On

Seventh Avenue we don't use strategy. The guy with the shortest reaction time wins, that's all. I copy other people's fashions. I've got this fantastic contract pattern maker who knows how I operate. I've got a cutter down the block who's worked with me five years now and knows the system. I've got this terrific sewing contractor in New Jersey who took me three years to break in. Over the last fifteen years, I've trained my shipping room manager, my salesman, and my bookkeeper to do it my way. And I've got the fastest reaction time in the district."

Mike is a scratch golfer, a devastating bridge player, a consistent winner at poker. And he has a hell of a long-range plan going for him too. *His* long-range plan has been systematically built around zero investment and seven people including him. His strategic objective has been to build an organization with an incredibly fast reaction time, with complete flexibility, with unquestioned loyalty, with perfect mastery of "his system," and with a very low breakeven point. Mike has been in the knock-off business for 15 years now and has always managed to make a good living in what is a thoroughly vicious, competitive, unforgiving environment. He attributes his success to the fact that he works every other Saturday. I think it's because he has a cleverly conceived, sharply focused, and well-implemented plan for his industry. He carries it around in his hip pocket and calls it "reaction time." Big deal. Mike is just an unsurpassed, closet-case strategic planner.

> SPRUCE UP THE ORACLE,
> DUST OFF THE BONES;
> BETTER GET READY
> 'CAUSE HERE COMES
> THE CROWD

Nothing sells like the future. From the Mesopotamians who searched their celestial omens, to the Greeks who consulted oracles, to the Romans who examined sheep entrails, to Manhattanites reading Jeanne Dixon in the *New York Daily News*, the world beats a path to the door of the diviner who does it better. If you want to generate interest, just announce a seminar on forecasting (particularly one in which you will unveil the latest variant of the Box–Jenkins forecasting model). It's the 1980's version of the old-fashioned medicine show. Step right up, step right up.

Is there a soul so crew cut and so rational as not to harbor some tiny yearning in a hidden corner for The Answer? Or Even A Peek? *Everybody* is a sucker for a sure tip on the future. The number of otherwise skeptical managers who would not believe their own mother if she told them that the sun will rise tomorrow, but who believe, as if in the Grail, that somewhere a forecasting model of unerring accuracy exists, defies count (and logic). If the mythical model existed, managerial life would be a problem in arithmetic (at worst a linear regression); economics would be a breeze; and reward would be reduced to the riskless rate of return on investments, the latest T-bill quote. (The implications of such a model for job security among forecasters and executives seem to be the one aspect that its avid seekers have overlooked.)

I sometimes wonder if man's urge to predict the future is biological, like the urge to sleep, eat, and spindle, fold, and mutilate computer punched cards. How else can I explain the behavior of otherwise serious, rational human beings rushing to the precipice of the unknown future and leaping off on the wings of an unqualified prediction in full view of the world? "People who predict don't know, or don't know they don't know."[3] They never quit either. A silly sampler follows, documenting the unquenchable human urge to extrapolate absolutely wrong conclusions about the future from the past. Paul Dickson, author of *The Future File*, collected these groaners. May we learn from them.

Manhattan

By the year 1900, Brooklyn undoubtedly will be the city, and Manhattan will be the suburb. Brooklyn has room to spread; Manhattan has not. The New Yorker uptown on 35th Street already finds it a tedious and annoying job to commute to his business downtown and home again. Can you imagine him fighting his way all the way up to the pig farms on 100th Street 40 years hence?

—*George Templeton Strong,*
1865

The West

I have never heard of anything, and I cannot conceive of anything more ridiculous, more absurd, and more affrontive to all sober judgment than the cry that we are profiting by the acquisition of New Mexico and California. I hold that they are not worth a dollar!

—*Daniel Webster, Senate*
speech, 1848

Aviation

The demonstration that no possible combination of known substances, known forms of machinery, and known forms of force can be united in a practical machine by which man shall fly long distances through the air, seems to the writer as complete as it is possible for the demonstration of any physical fact to be.

—*Simon Newcomb,*
astronomer, 1903

Population

The population of the earth decreases every day, and, if this continues, in another 10 centuries the earth will be nothing but a desert.

—*Montesquieu, 1743*

World Collapse

My figures coincide in fixing 1950 as the year when the world must go to smash.

—*Henry Adams, 1903*

The Atomic Bomb

That is the biggest fool thing we have ever done. . . . The bomb will never go off, and I speak as an expert in explosives.

—*Admiral William D. Leahy to President Truman, 1945*

The Brave New World of 1980

Scientists convened for the "Technology Forecast for 1980 Conference" by the Polytechnic Institute of Brooklyn in October, 1969 predicted:

Automated highways on which cars will travel safely in heavy traffic at high speeds without driver control.

Undersea hotels and resorts.

Such universal use of computerization that man's brain will finally be freed for pure research rather than even sophisticated mechanical use.

Orbiting factories in space.

(Reprinted with permission from "It'll Never Fly, Orville: Two Centuries of Embarrassing Predictions," *Saturday Review*, December 1979, page 36.)

Fortunately there has never been a forecasting model that can make a silk purse out of a sow's ear. Putting it differently, no forecasting model using data and relationships derived from past behavior, as they all do, can ever forecast *anything* that was not experienced in the past or any behavior pattern occurring for the first time. As Edmund Burke once wrote, "You can never plan the future by the past."

In our hunger for certainty, we ignore this hard truth. We stubbornly resist making peace with uncertainty and the inevitability of change. I'm persuaded that Arthur Schlesinger, Jr., captured the essence of this issue when he said,

> The technological model dominates the con-
> temporary imagination. Without fully grasping the
> indeterminacy of scientific law, we assume that we
> can predict the social and political future as accu-
> rately as we can predict an eclipse of the sun. This
> certitude underlies the cult of the expert. It can be the
> source of infinite trouble.[4]

Sadly, if you want to rely solely on forecasting (instead of on long-range planning), you must by definition limit your sphere of activity to highly repetitive, well-researched, low-level, modest rate-of-return kinds of decisions. Nothing wrong with doing so. There are plenty of repetitive, mundane activities that provide a lot of jobs to a lot of people and make money for organizations to boot. My point is this: if you're going to substitute forecasting for good long-range planning, be certain that you stay in a very predictable environment with very low rates of change, and be particularly sure that you don't bet big money on things beyond the short run. "The hell you say." OK, let me introduce you to what one very smart man says to the point.

ENTER P.D.

As Peter Drucker is fond of reminding people, "human beings can neither predict nor control the future. If anyone still suffers from the delusion that the ability to forecast beyond the shortest time span is given to us, let him look at the headlines of yesterday's paper and then ask himself which of them he could possibly have predicted ten years ago."[5]

For starters, could you have *forecasted* ten years ago that by today, a nation not among the superpowers, for example, India, would have the nuclear capacity to build and test an atomic bomb? Could you have *forecasted* ten years ago that the OPEC nations would by today have mounted and sustained a cartel capable of bringing the world to its knees? Could you have *forecasted* at the end of World War II that West Germany, then completely bereft of economic vitality, would become the strongest country, economically, in Western Europe, as well as perhaps the most politically stable? Could you have *forecasted* ten years ago our new romance with mainland China?

"Foul," you cry, "these are all examples of big stuff, economic and political trends on a grand scale that of course we can't predict." Then how about these practical, everyday business life examples, little stuff that we *can* forecast—right? Could you have forecasted 20 years ago that numerically controlled machine tools would produce over 75 percent of parts output in U.S. industry? Could you have forecasted 15 years ago that prebuilt roof trusses (which everyone thought were cheapies that would fall down) would today have replaced stick-built rafter roofs in the United States? Or (watch this hammerlock) could you have forecasted 10 years ago that foreign imported cars would not only account for one fifth of U.S. sales (with four foreign automakers ahead of American Motors in U.S. market share) but also dominate and set the styling and engineering standards for the entire U.S. automotive industry?

"Come on, Levin, all these technical developments— you're not playing fair." OK, then, let's look at some human things. Ten years ago could you have forecasted that conventional types of hierarchical organizations would have given way in many companies to "matrix" forms or "project team" organizations? Could you have forecasted the enormous rise of flex-time working hours in industry, or the relative decline of power-dominated leadership styles, or the effect of race discrimination as well as reverse discrimination cases on hiring and employment practices?

Don't feel whipped. Peter Drucker would say that this is exactly how the world always behaves. I believe him. The point is not to "forecast" change before it happens. (We might as well try to resurrect the oracle at Delphi or have a go at sheep entrails.)

FORECASTING:
WHO IN THE HELL HID
THE TEA LEAVES?

Long-range planning is not the identical twin of forecasting. To understand the true relationship between long-range planning and forecasting, we need to recall that forecasting extrapolates an answer from past experience—for example, how many home computers will sell next Christmas at Radio Shack—relevant only within the shortest time intervals. (And they're getting shorter every year.) Long-range planning, on the other hand, tells us what to do when we can't forecast.

There is one other difference. Forecasting tries to tell how things will turn out, even to providing us with a set of probabilities that certain future events will occur. *But what if we want to change the probabilities?* It is the unique province of top management to apply sufficient entrepreneurial insight to do exactly that, to change the probabilities that certain events will occur. Then, and only then, does our society reward managerial behavior appropriately. Like taking a bird dog with us into the field, we shape long-range plans to control timing and give ourselves improved odds of meeting our objectives. But closing the gap is the hunter's job, not the dog's. If we're lousy shots (don't know how to close the gap), it ain't the dog's fault. Even the best dog can't fly as fast as the birds. Moral: To change the probabilities that we'll up the mortality rate of quail this year, we incorporate target practice in our bird-hunting strategy.

Planning is an active attempt to *control* outcomes; forecasting by comparison is the more passive attempt to *predict* outcomes. Forecasting is concerned with making educated guesses about the future—technically supported educated guesses computer-aided educated guesses—but still guesses. Long-range planning, on the other hand, is concerned with deciding which specific courses of action organizations ought to take for the future. Thus, forecasting is a part of long-range planning, a necessary tool, but only one of several interdependent parts that make long-range planning work. Yes, Virginia, experts do their best, but, sadly, they're up against something bigger than they are.

OK, SIGN ME UP
FOR ONE LONG-RANGE PLAN.
AND NOW TELL ME, GENIUS,
WHAT DOES IT HAVE TO DO
WITH THE FUTURE?

Not what you think. Long-range planning does *not* deal with future decisions. It deals with the effect on our organization's future of decisions we make—or choose not to make—*today*. Like George Allen's decision to trade away raw recruits and future draft picks for old warriors that he knew could go out and play winning football *this* Sunday, the choices we make today change the choices available in years to come. (Like maybe no draft choices year after next.)

Given that an executive knows what the goals are, he or she is concerned with good decisions right now. The executive charged with developing company strategy for the late 1980s is not interested now in what he or she should do in 1989. Hell, all that person has to do is wake up on February 18, 1989, make a few phone calls, look out the window, and he or she will see precisely what he or she should be doing on that day.

The real questions that face executives concerned today with developing good competitive strategy for 1989 are three:

1. What should we do today to get ready for an uncertain 1989?
2. To what extent are today's decisions circumscribing our freedom to act in 1989?
3. To what extent are decisions we choose *not* to make today circumscribing our freedom to act in 1989?

WHAT SHOULD WE DO TODAY
TO GET READY FOR AN
UNCERTAIN 1989?

We get the best intelligence we can on present trends and critical variables—we look out into the future as best we can with all our experts (or other divining gear) to see what we can see. We then bring back the implications of what we see for today's behavior; we decide what effect these implications ought to have on the present direction we are taking. Then, if we think that a change is in order, we make it. If not, our planning has confirmed our present strategy.

Look at my friend in High Point, North Carolina, a manufacturer of fancy wooden veneers used to face furniture. He looks all around him today and sees artificial printed veneers, plastic panels painted to look like wood, and half a hundred new attempts to substitute synthetic materials for real wood and make them look as good in a home. He has access to sales figures on real and synthetic veneers for the last 20 years. He has several forecasts of real and synthetic veneer sales for the next 10 years or so. He sees from his past data and his forecasts that synthetics are commanding a greater share of the total market and that their share is growing on the order of something like 1.2 percentage points a year. He calculates that by 1989 synthetic veneer will account for 82 percent of the total market. This leaves producers of wood veneers with 18 percent of the market, or something on the order of $22 million. Because his sales are around $3 million annually, and because he is only the third largest among a number of smart, aggressive, well-organized industry members, he'd better figure that the size of the market in 1989 for wooden veneers may not be sufficient to sustain his company along with the rest of the hungry crew. Having confirmed that he should reexamine his current strategy in this manner, he cancels his golf game for today and begins to look harder at the Latin American lumber importing business he's had in the back of his mind for a year or two.

TO WHAT EXTENT
ARE TODAY'S DECISIONS
CIRCUMSCRIBING OUR
FREEDOM TO ACT IN 1989?

Every time an executive decides to take one course of action, some alternative course of action by definition is foregone—"the road not taken." (Luckily for top executives today, accountants still have not become adept at "make-good" audits and reports on opportunities foregone.) Each decision we make puts us either into a more flexible or into a less flexible position with respect to the future, or else it doesn't change our future flexibility at all. Unfortunately, however, present-day decisions, efficient for now but limiting flexibility later on, usually are judged by their present-day effect, whereas the extent to which they mortgage the future goes unnoticed.

I have a friend in Mississippi in the corrugated steel pipe business, the kind that's used for culverts under highways. Corrugated steel pipe is manufactured in either of two ways, annular or spiral. The annular method takes a flat sheet of steel, uses a lot of labor to put those funny corrugations in it, rolls it into a cylinder, and then rivets the edge together. The spiral method uses a very fancy machine costing about $250,000 (but requiring very little labor) to turn out corrugated pipe at fantastic speeds, like the machine that makes the roll inside paper towels.

So in an industry that operates at roughly 60 percent of present capacity, and with the major U.S. highway program 95 percent finished, my friend has chosen to invest in spiral machines. He currently has two of them. It's a cinch that his direct production costs will look good this year (if you leave out depreciation, that is). But I frankly wonder if his machine-buying decision derived from the sensible long-range planning that asks, what does this investment action today cause me to forego in freedom to act in 1989? What would half a million dollars today—or sometime in the next few years—have bought my Mississippi friend in the way of diversification to face 1989 in the uncertain corrugated pipe industry? I'm sure that he knows where he wants to be this year and next year. And he can forecast a couple of years out what the industry will do. But five years from now? Ten? Could be that my Mississippi friend just loves George Allen.

TO WHAT EXTENT ARE
DECISIONS WE CHOOSE NOT
TO MAKE TODAY
CIRCUMSCRIBING OUR
FREEDOM IN 1989?

Biting the bullet on time, particularly a big, strategic bullet, does not always bring fame to an executive. When your balance sheet looks sick, when the banks are baying at the back door, when the investors are in revolt, and when your stock's down ten points, it's hard to stand tall at the stockholders' meeting and assure everyone that good times are coming in 1987 as a result of the current deprivation. It takes real effrontery to tell them, moreover, that their present anguish is all according to plan, fear not and take the long view. As a matter of fact, it's an act almost impossible to pull off in a publicly held company. Bullet biting, while honorable and sensible, has political shortcomings that tarnish its popularity as an executive game. In private companies, though not painless, biting the bullet in a timely fashion is more easily done. Two examples: one that did, one that didn't.

First, let's look at Deering Milliken Corporation of Spartanburg, South Carolina, one of the largest privately held companies in the world, perhaps the third largest textile company in the United States today. Years ago it became apparent to Milliken's top management that the effective use of the computer was not easily or casually obtained. Looking around at others who used the computer, Milliken executives saw that lack of a dialogue between computer specialist and computer user was a major pitfall. It was also apparent to Milliken's management that, unless some real solution was found to this problem, the firm's future in computers was mortgaged for years to come—in incorrect hardware and software choices, in operating inefficiencies, and in personnel problems.

Having made this assessment, Milliken embarked on an ambitious long-range staffing strategy of rotation. Operating managers from Milliken's manufacturing division were cycled through the computer center for tenures of up to three years. More noteworthy, managers of the computer center who had achieved success in that endeavor were transferred to operating divisions and given manufacturing and marketing responsibilities. The effects of this cross-fertilization were astounding. True, this bullet biting cost a great deal of money (are you listening, George Allen?). But, as early as 1962, Deering Milliken had achieved success with its substantial computer investment unparalleled in the industry at that time. This superiority has continued for many years. Being privately held, management found it easier to take the hard road early at great expense in time and money. But the investment paid very well. Leadership was a contributing factor in Milliken's favor. Roger Milliken, head of the company, is a strong-willed man of whom it has been said that he would (and probably could) part the Red Sea again if he thought the return on investment would be great enough.

On the other hand, there is the case of Cone Mills. Cone, in Greensboro, North Carolina, started turning out denim for farmers' overalls in 1895, following this with cordurory in 1927. Today, these two fabrics account for 60 percent of Cone's $650-million annual sales. Exacerbating dependency on two products is Cone's further dependency on one major customer—Levi Strauss—which accounts for 20 percent of Cone's annual sales.

The fortunes of denim and cordurory have ebbed and flowed for 50 years. After World War II demand was high for women's denim and duckcloth pedal pushers, but the advent of motorcycle toughs (with jeans their trademark) precipitated a drop-off in demand. The president of Cone Mills Marketing

Company says, "We suffered through the 50's in demand for cotton denim. Then came the hippies with the natural lifestyle reflected in the overalls and the jeans adopted both as a uniform and an anthem of the times." Denim demand soared. The look was co-opted by respectable consumers, denim went uptown, decorators did sofas in it, designers turned it into $75 pairs of pants. But in 1978 another serious downturn in demand for denim impacted on Cone's bottom line. By the last half of 1978, denim prices had stabilized as a lot of companies stopped making the fabric.[6]

Cone Mills is a classic case of an organization apparently choosing not to make a strategic decision to diversify and willing to live with the reduction of freedom in 1989 that limited product dependency implies. They've lived life on a seesaw so long that apparently they don't mind the motion.

What's the evidence that not making the diversification decision over the last 20 years has been bad or good? Or that it has unduly constrained future freedom or earnings? (1) Cone is still in business after 85 years of a very limited product strategy. (2) Cone gets investor support for this strategy. (A textile analyst for Merrill Lynch said that Cone "enjoys a specialized niche. The less often you have to change a machine to produce other goods, the more efficient you are.") (3) A competitor described Cone as a "credible outfit" but argued that "with denim and corduroy accounting for so much of Cone's production, the lack of flexibility and the fact that they are so highly specialized can make Cone vulnerable to market shifts." (4) Recent press releases have indicated that Russia and China are interested in buying denim and (5) that Cone got almost a quarter of its sales from overseas markets last year.

Summing up, it looks to me as if Cone has survived in a modestly successful financial manner for a long time in spite of its *not* making the diversification decision. As Cone survives more and more market shifts without changing its basic limited product strategy, it probably feels tougher about the chances of doing so forever. Meanwhile, the president of Cone Mills recently said, "The company was looking for acquisitions, something good, profitable, and with its own management, but after about a year of looking we haven't seen anything that really excites us." Recall that in the story of the boy who cried wolf, the wolf finally did come down from the hills one day. If Cone chooses not to buy itself wolf repellent now, the fur may fly in Greensboro in 1989.

DOES LONG-RANGE PLANNING
TRY TO ELIMINATE RISK?

Rise up ye legions of truth and righteousness and strike down forever this terrible misconception. The grand old man of management philosophy, Peter Drucker, is adamant on this point: "It is not even an attempt to minimize risk."[7]

Risk taking, as the old farmer said, is what puts the bread on the table. This is a basic tenet of freshman economics. Risk is rewarded by an appropriate return. It is an axiom that reducing risk reduces returns on capital. Surely, then, the purpose of long-range planning cannot be to reduce return on investment. Far from it. Long-range planning is undertaken to make sure that the risks that the organization is taking are the right kinds of risks. In planning we seek to know enough about the future consequences of today's risk taking to be reasonably satisfied that we are doing the right thing today.

If analysis of present strategic decisions indicates that the inherent risks are too high, of course it is reasonable to alter the course of action to reduce risk to an acceptable level in the organization. On the other hand, the essence of successful entrepreneurial behavior is to take greater risks, not lesser risks. Consequently, for an entrepreneurially oriented company, it is highly appropriate to use long-range planning to increase its ability to take sensible risks.

My friend Stan is an oil jobber in southern California. He leases gas stations, buys gas from a major oil company, and retails it to people like you and me. Last year Stan did $6 million of business on a total investment of slightly less than

$100,000. He delights in showing me his balance sheet. (And I, in turn, horrify my risk-averse MBA students by showing it to them.) Stan has a current ratio of .85 and a debt-to-equity ratio of 8.5. Then, just out of pure meanness, I show the MBAs his income statement from last year: a 128 percent return on equity. Absolutely wipes them out. Can't understand it, they say. Simple, I say. Stan sees the oil industry as a big gamble. He doesn't want any of his money invested in it now or later. He can get no-recourse financing on his debt so he takes all he can get. He runs a tight ship. And his money runs so fast you can't tell whether it's printed green or blue. But, my MBAs say, isn't that *risky?* Damn right, I reply, but how can you get a 128 percent return on equity and still run it like a bank? I'd put old Stan up against any long-range planner I know today—a whole planning staff even—for having thought up a very appropriate long-range plan for himself and for realizing that a plan does not eliminate risk, it only lets you know more accurately what you have to sweat about to merit a 128 percent return.

OK, I GIVE UP, WHAT IS IT THEN?

It isn't forecasting, it's not concerned with future decisions, and it's not an attempt to eliminate risk. (And, as you may have inferred already, in Steve Allen's words, it's also "bigger than a breadbox.") Let's return to a man whom I respect tremendously. We can derive a common sense answer from Peter Drucker: *Long-range planning is the process of making current risk-taking decisions with the best possible knowledge of their future consequences.* (If this had already occurred to you independently the last time you stood at the 6,288-foot summit of Mt. Washington in your hang glider ready to leap, congratulations. Short-run applications are encouraged. Peter Drucker would approve.)

"Doing is believing," according to my precocious niece.

Or, as Napoleon would exhort you at this point (stirringly), "En avant, mes enfants! Marchons!" All of which translates to, hop on the bus for Chapter 3 and let's make a long-range plan.

NOTES

[1]Winston S. Churchill, *Second World War,* Volume 1, *The Gathering Storm* (Boston: Houghton Mifflin, 1948), p. 476.

[2]James Brian Quinn, "Strategic Goals: Process and Politics," *Sloan Management Review,* Fall 1977.

[3]John Kenneth Galbraith quoted by Adam Smith, "John Kenneth Galbraith in Person and Print," *New York Times Book Review,* September 30, 1979.

[4]A. Schlesinger, Jr., "The Futility of Futurism," *The Wall Street Journal,* December 12, 1977.

[5]Peter Drucker, "Long-Range Planning, Challenge to Management Science," paper presented to the Fourth International Meeting of the Institute of Management Sciences, Detroit, October 17-18, 1957.

[6]Barbara Ettorre, *The New York Times* Wire Service, June 17, 1979.

[7]Drucker, *op. cit.*

THREE

The Long-Range
Planning
Process

Seven steps to fame
and fortune . . . same tune,
different verse.

Nothing is more terrible than activity without insight

Thomas Carlyle

GARBAGE IN, GARBAGE OUT.
CAVEAT: INPUTS VERSUS
OUTPUTS (OFTEN CONFUSED)

Actually doing a long-range plan is both deceptively easy and incredibly tough! There hasn't been much argument in the last 20 years about the steps that one goes through in making a plan. But steps are a trapping of *form*, not of *substance*, and substance is what we're after in our long-range plan. Unfortunately, the easy part of long-range planning is going through the steps. Planners are human too; they don't mind falling into the lazy habit of going through the motions to satisfy form requirements. But doing so dodges the real conceptual task—creatively narrowing the strategic choices open to the organization.

Suffice it to say that jumping through hoops is not long–range planning. A commitment to following steps rather than to making strategic choices is a dangerous love affair with *inputs* (pages filled, figures neatly arranged, the "right" number of planning meetings held, the plan delivered precisely on time, colored tabs for easy access to sections, lots of pro formas, and other such minutiae). Moral: A four-color chart doth not a planner make (nor a pinstripe suit a banker). It's the *thought* that counts.

Some years ago, my dean, Maurice Lee, initiated a broadly based study of adult education at the business school. Committees were formed, meetings scheduled for the whole year, faculty hearings held, and opinions received and recorded. Toward the end of the academic year (a point in scholarly life where all creative organizational thought stops for three months), it became clear that what we had was a beautifully designed, broadly based, democratic system of *inputs*—and that was *all* we had. A joke without the punchline. A tickle in the nose without a sneeze. Where was the *output*?

Academics are fond of being late rather than wrong. (The ignominy of being rebutted in a scholarly journal, when another year or so of research and contemplation can avoid it, is more than a body can bear.) So it was natural for our faculty to feel that the task had been appropriately handled. Not Maurice! With one weekend left, he picked five faculty members and announced that he'd just made a reservation for two nights for us at a nearby conference center. Being a man of practical wisdom, he also announced that the school would pick up the liquor tab for our retreat. Three days later we returned with a brief (three-page) long-range plan for adult education—and I must add that it stood the school in good stead for ten years.

A good long-range plan emphasizes outputs not inputs, conceptual processes not formats, and, above all, prescription not description. It's not too hard to figure out where we are and to illustrate the position with nifty charts, but it takes creativity to decide wisely where we ought to go and how we ought to get there.

Remember, people with list-oriented mentalities have greater utility to companies as auditors than as planners. Planners are paid to throw away the list, get out from under the daily grind, gaze at the world around them, think original thoughts about what the company should do in that world, and tell the company how it could accomplish those objectives.

AGENDA

From here on out in Chapter 3, we'll be talking about how to do it. We'll use the format of a long-range plan to develop the planning process (avoiding dangerous love affairs with format, of course). Keep in mind, however, that operational considerations in long-range planning are the subject of a separate chapter, Chapter 4. If you find yourself wondering about timing, horizons, centralized and decentralized planning, bottom–up and top–down planning, inside–out and outside–in planning, these and like issues are

43

treated in more detail in the next chapter. Also, Chapter 5 is devoted entirely to behavioral aspects (rewards, planning styles, risk taking, participation, ownership, and much more), so these matters will be touched on lightly if at all at this point. As to form, I hold no doctrinaire view of what belongs in the body of the plan and what in an appendix—those are inputs and don't amount to a hill of beans.

Once More with Feeling

. . . and then we're off. We begin with the definition derived with Peter Drucker's help. *Long-range planning is the process of making current risk-taking decisions with the best possible knowledge of their future consequences.* In operation, the process works this way. Management reassesses its current strategy at the same time looking for opportunities and threats in the environment over some future time period—anywhere from one to twenty years out, let's say. By balancing these opportunities and threats against the organization's strengths and weaknesses, management can illuminate several strategic alternatives. Management evaluates each possible strategy against the organization's objectives. Then, selecting a strategy (or confirming the present strategy), management implements it through a series of shorter-term action plans. That's it. Now that we have it in a nutshell, let's move on to step 1 of how to do a long-range plan.

STEP 1: THE HISTORY SECTION OF A LONG-RANGE PLAN

Capturing Equity for the Organization: Every long-range plan should embark with some history of the organization. Aside from leavening the inherent vicariousness of forecasts, it actually adds value to the planning process—like helping the organization to avoid making the same stupid mistake it made back in 1963. All organizations accumulate *equity*, not the kind on the right side of the balance sheet, but another kind with value denominated in other than dollars. The other equity consists of personal knowledge about how things run around here. Its equity value is the sum of memories about what you tried four years ago and lost your shirt on, the equity value of knowing what your predecessor knew that you didn't when he screwed up the organization that you're now trying to unravel, the equity value of knowing how the competition generally responds, and even the simpler equity value of knowing where things are kept, which ones you use in different situations, and why the circuit breaker trips when you change from heat to air conditioning without disconnecting the electric incinerator first.

 The first job I had out of college was in a brassiere factory as an industrial engineer. (I never wondered about my calling more than the day the president of the company came into the receiving department, where I was working on what I thought was a very complex problem—more about which in a moment—and said, "Dick, you're an engineer, can't you do something about these flies?") Anyhow, two energetic young men, Toby and Aaron, took care of the receiving warehouse in this company. Each day with great dispatch they received, accounted for, and put away (in locations known only to them) thousands of yards of different kinds of lace, hundreds of boxes of different buckles for bra straps, truckloads of fabric in all textures and colors, and a myriad of other materials used in bra construction. I had been assigned to study the receiving warehouse's efficiency. (Efficiency was a word to which I responded then like Pavlov's dog.) Hell, I thought, the efficiency is terrific, just Aaron and Toby running the whole thing. Aaron got drafted on July 14, 1951, and Toby's appendix came out two days later. There it was—the whole receiving staff equity gone at one stroke. It was a week before anybody could find enough material of one kind to start the plant again. That was the week I got my first lesson in how to capture equity for the organization. I still remember it. (I remember the flies more, though!)

The Collective Memory,
or Somebody Go Ask the Old Guy
with the White Beard
Who's Been Here Since 1923

Capturing what we've done in the past helps to ensure continuity in strategic thought. (Notice, however, I did not imply that continuity is the most desirable characteristic of a good long-range plan—only that it's useful.) If we can retain the equity of the executives who've preceded us, our plan is the better for it. We gain perspective on the present when we can see the direction or thust of company strategy prior to the immediate past, the last few years. Remember that other people will read and use our plan. As the kids say, they need to know where we're coming from.

External and Internal Histories
(You Thought There Was
Only One?)

It will be useful to include in the history section of your plan a brief summary of the major trends in the external environment. You will have to be your own judge of how far to pursue this line. Sometimes it is worthwhile to get specific about past market behavior, including the organization's past strategy, past competitive conditions, and behaviors of certain significant competitors—expressed in dollar figures, percentages, and germane statistical measures. If so, this information will be most valuable if kept brief. (The same could be said of *all* information.)

Your internal history will convey an idea of how your organization has responded to the environment in the past. Use specific quantitative measures of success and failure. (Yes, failure—this is no place to blush while you're examining the organization naked in a mirror.) The standard litany of accounting and financial data is useful, as are measures of marketing performance—share of market, major product line age, and company sales growth rate versus industry growth rates—these are all useful.

You will find that, of all sections in a long-range plan, the history section is the easiest to write. (It is also the least useful.) Because it is easy, it also tends to be long and given to clever but administratively useless backslapping over past success. Resist this temptation. Containing little or no uncertainty, the past is of limited value to you. (Remember the correlation of risk and return.) Pick up significant trends, measures, and decisions of the past, write them down, and get on with it. "How long?" you ask. "No universal parameters," I respond. "Aw, give us a hint." "OK, a few years ago I saw the long-range strategic plan for a major textile company with sales in the low billions annually. Its history section was neatly compressed into 5 pages out of 123 total pages—about right, I'd say." "Damn," you say, "but I know so much about it!" Yeah, but hindsight ain't sellin' these days, and you can't differentiate hindsight—everyone's is 20–20 by definition.

STEP 2: THE SIZE-UP SECTION OF A LONG-RANGE PLAN

How Tough Are We, Coach? In assuming the presidency, Franklin D. Roosevelt sized up how much courage and reserve people in this country had in 1932 better than the people could themselves. Later he

47

sized up the industrial potential of America prior to World War II better than the captains of industry could themselves. Winston Churchill (not a bad size-up artist himself) said that Roosevelt "anticipated history." The ability to size up situations quickly, accurately, and objectively has always been a hallmark of successful leaders.

Who and what are we sizing up? In our case, we're talking about sizing up the organization (which is us)—in other words, a "here's how tough we are" assessment. Here we must be concise, timely, situation-specific, and, above all, objective—always objective. Sizing up is not the place in the long-range planning process for dreaming, even for dreamers.

One of the best stories I've ever heard about the quick size-up concerned Ralph A. Hart, then president of Heublein, Inc. His leading brand, Smirnoff vodka, was enjoying enormous market success; it was "fully priced," well advertised and promoted, and making a mint of money for the company. One day, the story goes, one of Hart's less fearless lieutenants dashed into his office with the news that the competitive vodka had just reduced the price a dollar a fifth. "Should we cut Smirnoff a dollar too?" asked the nervous assistant. Hart paused a moment, then replied, "Hell no, raise the price a dollar and put it into advertising." A quick size-up of brand strengths and advertising elasticities indeed, but one that proved to be on the mark.

Counting Spearchuckers

It boils down to, how many we got? How many they got? Strategic planners (kings, generals, coaches) have asked this question from the beginning of time. "What king, going to make war on another king, sitteth not down first, and consulteth whether he be able with ten thousand to meet him that cometh against him with twenty thousand?" (*Luke*, 14:31). Nothing has changed—ask Avis.

Sizing up our organization demands an objective inventory of our resources in the broadest sense—capital availability, physical facilities, people, traditional organization strengths, market strength, and the like. It's critical for you as a planner to realize here that, like leases, many of a company's strengths do *not* appear on the balance sheet. With a few fledgling exceptions such as human resource accounting, people and organizational strength are not quantitatively measured. And yet, 50 years ago, Andrew Carnegie highlighted this reporting weakness when he said, "Take my railroads, take my millions, but leave me my organization and within a year I'll be back stronger than ever." (And he hadn't read the first word about human resource accounting.)

Many planners find it practical to size up using a functional area approach—how tough are we in marketing, finance, R & D, production, human resource management, and so on. I know a few others who lately have begun to size up for planning by using a more decision-oriented approach—how good are we at securing inputs, planning operations, evaluating alternatives, controlling outputs, reacting to change, and so on. Though less structured than traditional formats, the latter approach does put more emphasis on overall organizational strengths rather than on segmented functional area strengths. For that reason it merits consideration, especially for firms competing in a fast-moving marketplace.

Trio

Regardless of the size-up model you choose, do not forget these three ingredients: *symmetry, specificity,* and *visibility.* They go with sizing up any subject from any angle. Symmetry first—do you know any organization that has only strengths, no weaknesses? Or vice versa? Then it's simple logic to size up with a symmetrical look, balancing the two, strengths and weaknesses. So our production is extremely efficient and we have good control systems, but our distribution is weak in key market areas and our service is erratic and losing us customers. No time for false modesty as to strength or for blinders on weakness. Dissect both sides—that's symmetry.

Specificity—its value in sizing up can't be over-emphasized. Divisions, departments, persons—name them in assessing strengths and weaknesses. The *ad hominem* assessment has been common in lower-level planning for a long time; it's a more recent development for this specificity to be extended upward to assessments of executive strength, person by person, position by position. This is a useful trend.

Visibility—remember that much of who you are (your organization) and how tough you are will *not* be found in financial statements. Unless you know what you're looking for, you won't find it. The visibility of organizational strength is much harder to detect and measure than the visibility of financial strength, which people have been measuring for years; yet detecting organizational strength is much more important in determining outcomes. The point here is to use your imagination, your judgment, your intuition. You may have to invent your own measures; you certainly will have to use your eyes differently to perceive the different, off-balance sheet visibility of organizational strength at the human level.

STEP 3: ORGANIZATIONAL OBJECTIVES IN THE LONG-RANGE PLAN

What League Do You Want to Play in? My friend Stan in California is very happy playing in the 128 percent return-on-equity, high-risk league as an oil jobber. He instinctively discards all other "less attractive" (Stan's words) kinds of investments. Red Adair would love Stan.

On the other hand, my friend and colleague at the University of North Carolina, DeWitt Dearborn, is only happy fishing when he has two motors on his boat and stays within 100 feet of shore. DeWitt, therefore, automatically discards all but low-risk, low-yield investments.

Then there's Marcel Robins, a shopping center developer who lives up the street from me. He's middle league. Marcel isn't really happy until he has nine shopping centers under construction simultaneously, all with cost overruns, contractors' delays, leasing problems, and insufficient financing. Marcel tells me that for a 24 percent after-tax rate of return, you just can't beat the life!

Each of these persons has set objectives for rate of return, risk level, and attendant life-style, and each of them considers investment alternatives appropriate to these objectives. The key is knowing who you are (and that's the size-up, remember?). My friends Stan, DeWitt, and Marcel, know their own strengths and weaknesses, what they like to do best, and what risks they feel comfortable with. It sure saves time. Moral (you can thank Socrates for this one): Know yourself.

Onesies, Twosies, Threesies

Like my three friends, formal organizations choose objectives too. Some are quantitative—return on investment, share of market, growth rates. Others are qualitative but equally important—flexibility of the organization to withstand technological change, economic stability measured by how well the organization copes with the vagaries of business cycles, and organizational climate or what we want the personality of this company to be. And there are many others.

Objectives can come in twosomes, even threesomes. For example, an organization may decide that it wants a minimum return on investment of 15 percent coupled with a market share of not less than 10 percent. Or it might say that it wants to grow at 30 percent per year compounded, earn not less than 45

51

percent on equity, and finance this trip to the moon solely with internally generated funds. That's a threesome. (But in this case it doesn't matter what it is—it can't be done.)

Objectives as Fixed Screens—
Danger Ahead

Organizations ought to and often do change their objectives over time. As the organization feels itself growing stronger, it might well adjust its risk-taking objective upward to take advantage of alternative strategies offering higher rates of return. (Measures of increasing strength would be position in the industry, depth and quality of leadership within the organization at all levels, effectiveness of forecasting and control systems, financial position.) But life is symmetrical too—if the organization feels itself growing weaker, it's time to adjust objectives downward also.

The real mistake is the automatic use of objectives to screen out "inappropriate" alternatives. Nothing stays the same forever; it's stupid, then, to use a set of objectives as an automatic door opener to "appropriate" strategies way past the point where they have worn out. My colleague DeWitt Dearborn might just take a notion one day to cash in some Treasury bonds, buy a 25 foot Sea Ox boat and a 235 horsepower Johnson outboard, throw all caution to the winds, and race out 3 miles from shore. He has the choice, depending on how he feels, and so have formal organizations. As individuals within organizations grow and develop and take on more responsibilities, so might organizations within an industry. On the other side, as individuals "Peter Principle out," the organization must recognize when it's getting in over its collective head.

The reduction in thoughtful analysis, which seems to accrue to executives who use company objectives as a fixed screen, comes at a very high price. It's like trying to use a simple computer model to make executive decisions—works great until the environmental parameters change, as they say in the trade. There are still some things that have to be reflected on in a quiet, nonscientific way, and the choice of objectives (or their adjustment) is one of them.

STEP 4: FORECASTING
THE ENVIRONMENT IN THE
LONG-RANGE PLAN

Forecasting and Planning Revisited. In Chapter 2 we went to great pains to show that forecasting definitely is not long-range planning but that it is an important part of the long-range planning process. We perform forecasts to see if the environmental factors that permitted the organization's strategy to be successful in the past are as likely to continue. If not, we ask which new opportunities and risks must be evaluated at this time.

Let's put that another way. We look ahead to search the environment for changes that may impact on the strategy we're implementing today. (Remember, the Mississippi corrugated steel pipe maker? The big change in his environment was the winding down of interstate highway construction.) We do this search with all humility about the frailties of forecasting methods and with full knowledge of the capriciousness of the environment; nonetheless, we still do it because we must. Partial knowledge is better than no knowledge at all, and a good planner works with whatever is available.

The minimum bet we make as planners at this stage is (1) that we can see *some* things coming, (2) that we can *sometimes* see how fast they're coming, and (3) that as to the things we see coming pretty fast we can at least *speculate* on their meaning for our present strategy. Make no mistake, forecasting the environment farther than a little way out is rarely more elegant or successful than that. But planners never stop doing it. It's a little like grand slams in bridge, rare indeed, but the rarity doesn't stop bridge players from playing, or from winning with just the normal run of the cards (and a good strategy).

But What Do We Watch for, Coach?

Bill Fischer, a professor in the Business School at Chapel Hill, has a lot of evidence that you can forecast changes in the technological environment with some success. I haven't asked Bill about the other facets of the environment—economic, political, social—but my hunch is that, of these, changes in technology may be the most easily forecastable, followed by changes in the economy, politics, and society, in that order. (You may have your own preferred order, equally valid, from any of the 23 mathematically possible combinations. The only certainty is that even the "easiest" is damn tough.)

Nuts, Bolts, and Switches

If you were interested in forecasting your technological environment, Bill would suggest that you pay attention to patents awarded, to published technical papers, to data on performance of technologies already in use, to financial support and changes in financial support underwriting technological research, to topics presented at technical meetings, and to reports on the progress of developing technologies. Half joking, I advise my clients at Duke Power Company to keep their eye on the development of amorphous silicones ("glassy switches," as they're called), devices that transform light directly into electricity. Although my own gut forecast is that it will be at least 15 years before this technology becomes commercially feasible, I enjoy seeing my Duke Power friends get antsy over the thought of obsoleting billions worth of generating facilities, poles, and wire. It's a good drill once in a while for high-salaried executives to get nervous about things like that. It may even plant the seed of thought that what looks like a monster problem might be turned into a competitive opportunity. Happily, the recent announcement of a government-sponsored electric power project in the American desert using only amorphous silicones to generate power for an Indian village makes me somewhat less of a nut in my friends' eyes.

*Doing Dismally at the Dismal
Science*

Planners taking a shot at economic forecasting find a flood of methodologies and data available. For about $15,000, you can have the Chase Econometric Forecast, and, if that straps you, you can slide down the scale all the way to "freebies" and other inexpensive publications available from the government. For $5 there's even a spiritualist located on the highway between Selma and Four Oaks, North Carolina, who will do a 15-minute forecast, and she doesn't even have a terminal in her living room. (Don't laugh, her record is only slightly less laudable than the last three economic advisors to the President.)

Chapter 7 of this book contains 88 standard sources available today for economic forecasting with comments about each. Suffice it to say here that forecasting the economic environment is best done at three levels: *internal*—production costs, facility costs, capital costs, resource costs, and the like; *external*—demand, markets, product life cycles, price behaviors, industry capacities, product loyalties, entries and exits; and *international*—macrochanges or evidence of impending changes in trade volumes, comparative advantage, basic resource shifts, developing markets, barriers to trade, capital availability, political climates, and a myriad of others. Think where you'd be today if you'd forecasted the OPEC cartel's power before its members tightened the noose. (Now *that's* a grand slam.) You don't like oil, then what about gold prices?

Dewey Beats Truman?

Forecasting the political environment is harder but lots more fun. (Nothing is too silly to be given national credibility—like speculation that a powerful Democratic senator will try to wrest the party's presidential nomination from the Democratic incumbent, based on the senator's having given up ice cream.)

A big mogul in banking in Virginia did a long-range plan for his bank some years ago (before he became a big mogul). His plan was based on his own political forecast that the Virginia legislature would legalize branch banking in that state. His colleagues at the bank thought he was batty, but he claimed to have "signals" or political clairvoyance and planned away nonetheless. The result was a comprehensive plan for branch banking, not even legal at the time. He was rewarded for his amazing perspicacity by being made chief executive officer of the bank two years later when the legislature did what it would never do. When the bombshell dropped, and while all the other banks (and everybody in his bank too) were running around wondering what it would take to implement a branch-banking strategy, he had it all in his desk waiting. That's called "playing oracle." When you hit, you get rich and famous. When you miss you get passed over. It's a risky game, God knows, even in banks, but exhilarating as little else can be when you correctly call the future.

Political forecasting observes such indicators as election outcomes, political appointments, implied and express changes in national, state, and local goals, creation of new government agencies, regulatory activity, changes in the tax structures, formulation and dissolution of special interest and public interest groups, changes in the composition of governing bodies, changes in the courts and ice cream consumption by secretaries. A vast amount of political prognostication is free; and yours is probably as good as all but half of 1 percent.

Hamburgers and Cars

In the social environment, forecasters look at attitudes and values, and changes in these; at population and all the ingredients of demographic mixes; at mass behaviors such as consumerism; at crime, social conflicts, and other disorders; at attitudes toward work, leisure, education, and family life. It has been said that the fast-food phenomenon was eminently forecastable if one had had the good sense to use the proper sociological independent variable—namely, the rise in working women that created households in which two people worked and no one had time to cook. So where was my sociologist when McDonald's went public?

Social change in its time frame more resembles technological change than economic change, that is, the cycles or patterns are long in the making. Take, for instance, the issue of mass transportation in America. At the end of World War II, the country had a fairly good mass-transportation system (due in some measure to gas rationing during the war). With the economy booming, incomes rose rapidly, life-styles changed, and city living with its quick bus or trolley ride to the office or plant gave way to "that nice little house in the country" (and of course a car, maybe even two). Mass transportation was caught in a downward spiral—riders quit for cars, service became worse, more riders went to cars, and so on. The government built more and more roads, until the country was almost totally dependent on motor vehicles. By early 1979, over 90 percent of all travel was in private cars. That side of the cycle took a little over 30 years to complete. In the 1980's, as a result of *external* pressures and constraints, I believe that the country has embarked on the other side of the long cycle of change, that is, the change back to mass transportation, focused this time on energy conservation and alternative fuel sources. What a field day for the forecasters!

But It Ain't That Easy, Coach

I know! Some changes simply aren't perceptible to us at the right time. Others come on like a freight train too late to get ready for. Furthermore, so many pots are cooking in the environment at once that it's hard to decide what the significant indicators are to measure and monitor. And, once you do get all your technological, economic, political, and social data collected, does it give you a clear picture of where the environment is going—or even where it is? Hell, no. What you've got, very often, is a set of conflicting signals that leave you with no conclusion, or else too many. What then, coach? Well, sheep entrails are one possibility. I never said forecasting would be easy or precise.

STEP 5: ILLUMINATING AND EVALUATING STRATEGIC ALTERNATIVES IN THE LONG-RANGE PLAN

How It Works in Principle. What have we got so far in the planning process? We have our *history* of past efforts, we have a *size-up* of our capabilities, we have a statement of our *objectives*, and we have a *forecast* of what the environment is likely to bring. Obviously, we also know the nature of the organization's *present strategy* (multiple strategies in the case of diversified firms). Now we do two things:

1. We define the feasible alternative strategies that we might pursue—strategies that our size-up shows that we are tough enough or can become tough enough to tackle, and

2. We match each feasible alternative against our set of organizational objectives to see which one, or which combination, gives us the best overall level of performance.

(I know. It *sounds* so simple, like eating abalone at Scoma's in San Francisco. But someone had to get the boat ready, catch the abalone, clean it, tenderize it, sautee it, and bring it to the table looking simple and delicious. Moral: Never take a simple-looking abalone for granted—pay homage to the effort. I do, I do.)

How It Works in Practice

I have clients in the wholesale business currently doing about $120 million in annual sales. Over the last five years, the firm has grown at a 37 percent compound annual rate. The firm's profits after taxes is about 2 percent of sales, and the return is something on the order of 22 percent on equity. This past spring we went through the definition and evaluation of alternatives like this. The clients set out for me the dimensions of their *size-up:* they felt they had sufficient position strength, leadership, and knowledge of the marketplace to grow at virtually any unconstrained rate. With respect to company *objectives*, they stated their desire to keep their company private and in the same basic wholesaling market and to finance all future growth with retained earnings and bank debt. A further objective was to continue growing as rapidly as in the past for the indefinite future, with no diminution of earnings as a percentage of sales. They were also willing to operate with a maximum bank debt-to-equity ratio of .8. In terms of an *environmental forecast,* they persuaded me that given their reputation, the demographics of the marketplace, and the nature of the competition, there was little or nothing on the horizon for the next six to seven years likely to constrain growth or represent an unacceptable risk to them.

In this instance, the strategic alternatives were circumscribed by company objectives to growth rates in basically the same markets. It took less than half a day with a pro forma simulator to generate a set of outcomes combining their objectives. In this instance, I tried growth rates all the way from 20 to 40 percent over a six-year horizon. The results were dramatic (to them). The only *sustainable* growth rate meeting their financial objectives was something a bit less than 24 percent, or roughly two thirds of the previous growth rate. When the results were presented to the board of directors, one thing was certain: the planning process had *not* confirmed the continuation of their past strategy. In fact, continuation of their present growth rate (37 percent) would have resulted in a bank debt-to-equity ratio in six years of 1.8—completely intolerable to them—not to mention the fact that no bank would be about to lend them $56 million in 1986! The rest of the meeting quickly got turned around to rationing resources kind of talk—that is, which one of you heroes will have his horse reined in next year?

Not very many exercises in illumination and evaluation of alternatives turn out to be this structured or this simple, and practically none can be done in the short time that this one was. Many times, this step in planning ends up validating the present strategy. (This is particularly often the case in well-run, environmentally tuned organizations.) When a strategy review validates current strategy, it's a bad mistake to feel compelled to try something new. I've seen more sweet situations ruined when a good planning exercise validated previous strategy but some yo-yo in power insisted that doing the same old thing another year just couldn't be the right answer—and proceeded to kill the goose with a wild, unjustified strategic departure. Look at my friend Bill. He runs an aviation business in South Carolina. In 25 years, Bill has made good money doing what he does best, selling aircraft, running a large repair operation, and operating a flight school and charter business. If it's airplanes and engines, Bill knows it. Each year he takes a few days off, sits down, and assesses the future of his business. And, without exception, for the last 20 years, the message has been clear: fair skies, keep those planes flying, just do what you do so well. Yet, every few years Bill takes a notion. He says, "Dick, I'm tired of doing the same old thing." With that he cranks up some new unrelated venture (as if he had a fatal aversion to consistent profitability). The last scheme was an open-spaces multifamily residential development that lost him $300,000. The one before that was a tree forest for producing pulpwood (in five years they said. He was lucky there and got out only $120,000 behind.) So remember, if you lust for unrelated ventures outside your market and your competence, satisfy yourself with sex, sports, or the vicarious pleasures of *Fortune* magazine. But leave that golden goose alone.

A parting word on illuminating and evaluating alternatives. Be aware that the process of selecting strategic alternatives is not as economically objective in life as it appears to be in print. There is *no* place in the management of an enterprise in whch pure judgmet plays a more vital part than right here. If you don't have good judgment, tuning up the *process* just isn't going to get you there. For example, there's a Southern life insurance company at hasn't grown in ten years—and God knows that management has tried enough remedies. It has a heavily centralized long-range planning system with planning responsibility totally vested in the most phlegmatic, conservative, unimaginative, downright stupid man I've ever met. He, in turn, operates with the most detailed set of planning forms, deadlines, meeting schedules, rules, systems, and otherwise useless trappings ever collected. The planning *system* works magnificiently as a mechanical operation: management thinks that it does a whole lot of long-range planning. But the planning *process* is a bust; there's simply no room or time in it for judgment. So the only thing missing is thought—and that's everything. The company has a clerk's mind doing a thinker's job, and the outcome has been a sad but mechanically predictable one.

STEP 6. IMPLEMENTING
STRATEGY IN THE LONG-RANGE PLAN

The Gap and How to Close It, or What Will It Take to Get Us from Here to There? OK, Coach, now that the dog has found the birds, what do we do? If the long-range planning process to this point has validated past strategy, there is not much of a gap between what we're doing now and what we should be doing; therefore, the gap to be closed is not a significant one. Keeping the organization finely tuned on its present course is a process of making sensible modest corrections and adjustments. On the other hand, if our long-range planning process indicates that the present strategy is not appropriate, or worse, that it hasn't been appropriate for a long time now, then the gap between what we're doing and what we ought to be doing is a big one calling for significant time and effort to close. Having illuminated the gap is akin to having found the birds. If you like quail, they won't jump in your plate; you have to go get them. It's the same as abalone.

Closing Little Gaps

Defining the gap as a little one doesn't mean there's nothing more to do but light a cigar and think of your bonus. After all, if the gap *is* small, clearly somebody has been on the ball for some time now, and that usually means working his or her fanny off. If you're in good shape strategically, it's probably because you've been running hard and now is no time to stop—time to readjust your stride maybe, but not time to quit! Little-gap strategies usually require activities such as reducing costs, improving methods, tuning up the organization and reporting responsibilities, sharpening up control systems, improving and focusing training, sharpening market research and other environment signal-seeking methodologies, and the typical range of human resource management and development tactics. All these are aimed at doing a better job at what we're already doing. Daimler-Benz AG offers an excellent example. The German automaker, producer of the Mercedes-Benz, spends 8 to 10 percent of its sales on research and development. Current applications of constantly improving technologies are implemented daily on the plant floor—not in the next model year, but daily. Most such changes are minor, but the result is part of Daimler-Benz's strategy: "We give the customer a state-of-the-art car."[1]

Substrategies for closing little gaps are important, and plenty of organizations never learn this art of fine tuning, a form of professionalism. But, to a lot of people, keeping small gaps closed isn't half as exciting as changing strategic direction, whether it makes sense to do so or not. (Recall Bill in the aircraft business.) This behavioral problem is like trying to slow down your golf swing for consistency when you're really longing to kill the ball for a 250-yard drive. So getting in the groove isn't as much fun as bashing—I admit it. But getting in the groove wins more games—and that's more fun than losing. (In Chapter 5 we address this and other behavioral issues in greater detail.)

My friends in the wholesale business whom I mentioned earlier have a fairly big gap to close—throttling down their growth rate from roughly 37 percent to roughly 24 percent. Now there's an interesting gap! To close the gap, the major parts of their action plan would be these:

1. Financial: an action plan for rationing financial resources
2. Organizational: an action plan focusing on new hiring rates, intracompany transfers, and personnel reduction
3. Marketing: an action plan for controlling growth of markets in a move from extensive market exploitation to intensive development of fewer locations
4. Human Resources: an action plan detailing just how "being less successful," that is, growing less rapidly, is going to be sold to an organization now hell bent on growth—and successful at it

Of these four, the last is the toughest and probably the most important.

Each of these individual action plans is simply a detailed part of the organization's chosen strategic alternative, to pursue significant, but less rapid, growth. The individual action plans signify agreement on the implications of the overall plan for all areas, together with their proposed response. Each of these individual action plans contains more details about *outcome, speed,* and *timing*—that is, what are we going to do, when will we do it, and who will do it? This whole process of implementing action plans within a strategic long-range plan is referred to as "laying it off on the organization," and we will have more to say about "laying it off" in Chapter 5.

Big Gaps and Little Gaps, Twice the Work Load

Look back for a moment at the section on closing little gaps, particularly at the list of activities involved in that effort. These are all "fine-tuning" kinds of behaviors given a strategy that is appropriate. None of them represents an abrupt change of direction in that strategy; however, most or all of these "fine-tuning" behaviors are *also* necessary in the process of successfully implementing a change in strategic direction. If there's one thing that experience teaches us, it's that a mediocre strategy brilliantly implemented is infinitely better than a brilliant strategy indifferently implemented. (Just ask any really good sports writer about the relative value of the coach and the raw material in athletics.) What all this means, of course, for my friends in the wholesale business is that, while they are making some abrupt changes in basic company philosophy about growth rates and worrying about the biggies—financial resources, manpower reductions and shifts, refocusing marketing, and selling this whole idea to the organization—they must also keep their collective eye on the nitty-gritty, day-to-day activities of cost reduction, methods improvement, reporting and control systems, training, market research, forecasting capabilities, and human resource development. Otherwise their organization gradually will lose the vitality necessary to implement *any* strategy. Why-in-the-hell, you say, don't they just go public and get the money to do what they need to do? Foul, I cry, that's step 3 of the planning process, and they decided a long time ago that being private was a primary objective. Besides, we're getting ready to go into step 7. You should have thought of it then. Too late!

STEP 7: ODDS AND ENDS—
ASSESSMENT, REVIEW, AND
REPLANNING IN THE LONG-
RANGE PLAN

Q: How Long, Oh Lord? A: Long Enough. Once we have completed the long-range planning process, our problem becomes one of deciding when and how we should next change the strategic plan. ("If" is not generally a relevant question in the planning business.) In most organizations, strategic plans are reviewed at scheduled time intervals. The five-year plan is common, for example—no one knows where the five-year parameter came from—and is generally reviewed and updated annually. Making scheduled reviews is both good and bad. It's good in that it assures continued attention to the strategic planning process that, because of the nature of the environment, is a continuing process. It's bad to the extent that it invites long lapses in strategic planning activities between scheduled replanning sessions.

In larger organizations with planning staffs, the planning process does take on a continuous character, and this is some insurance against lapses. In smaller organizations, however, agreeing to look at the present plan again a year (or two) from now is kind of like buying stocks and putting them away until retirement. Unless you know precisely how to pick the growers and comers, you may want to look at what you're doing from time to time.

Things to Watch

I have a neighbor Walt down at the coast who lives about 500 yards up the beach. Whenever he starts catching pompano or flounder, I start moving his way. Think the competition's any different? Except, for you, it won't be fishing, it will be business, and the fact is that competitors' actions generally always threaten your strategic effectiveness. Competitors, therefore, like poaching fisherman, bear watching.

The same changes in technology that spawned your new strategy will eventually kill it—there is no greater planning truism than that. Therefore, technology bears very close watching indeed. The faster it moves, the faster you move. And you dare not limit your surveillance to events outside the organization either. Special internal competencies have a habit of being *ad hominem,* and, when your number one assistant Sam leaves, Sam generally takes his competence (and part of your strategic advantage) with him. And, of course, special internal competencies that are technology-based have predictable half-lives too; it's just not sane to bet your company fortune that no one will emulate your process.

Watch your organizational climate too. Organizations have a very definite capacity and need for taming alligators. If you underfeed this need, your people get disappointed and move on to better alligator ponds. If you overfeed the need, they get tired and sloppy and eventually may be eaten by the competitor's alligator.

Good Stuff, Coach,
But My Company
Just Ain't Big Enough
for All That

Complaints, complaints, complaints. Many owner-managers of smaller companies give long-range planning short shrift. There are lots of reasons for this: not enough time, other things are more important, too busy putting out fires, no staff to help me, I'm a doer not a planner, my good ideas are all secret

and I don't want to put them down on paper, I can react quickly enough to anything—and other assorted myths. To the harassed small-business executive with six or seven hats, all these complaints are real. Educators take two approaches to solving this problem. Some try to change the planning philosophy of a business person who by sheer dint of hard work and luck is worth a couple of million bucks by pointing out to him or her how going through this exercise will make him or her a better person. A crock, I say! Let's take the other approach: here's a very short, quick and dirty, highly abbreviated approach to long-range planning that won't take you very much time at all or reduce your profits, want to try it?

Commonsense Long-Range Planning
If You're Too Busy
to Do the Other Kind

Here it is, a simple process that doesn't take much time but gets at the guts of long-range planning nevertheless:

Step 1: Have your secretary retype the list below onto both sides of a 3″ × 5″ index card.[2]

What business am I in?
What is my place in the industry?
What customer am I serving?
What is my image to my customers?
Will my present market last another five years?
Do I need any plans to improve my products?
Do I want to grow; if so, how much?
How can I finance growth?
What share of the market do I want next year?
Do my employees operate well under my personnel policies; are they strong contributors to my success, my problems?
When was the last time I exposed myself to some new ideas about my industry; am I lazy about keeping up?

What's the biggest threat to my success—internal or external? Is it getting bigger or smaller, what can I do about it?

What is my greatest strength; do I use it fully?

What is my greatest weakness; am I doing anything to solve it?

Am I still having fun in this business?

How does the government and the public interest impact on me?

Does the public at large regard my business favorably; does it matter; if I need public goodwill, how can I communicate what I do and what I contribute to the public benefit?

Does my company have a strategy that I can actually put into words (other than some basic financial objectives)?

Are there any golden opportunities out there that nobody's noticed but me?

No "what-happens-if-I-die" kind of life insurance peddling questions. Just good commonsense planning-for-a-going-concern questions as in the list just given. (If you die, you die, so stop worrying about it.)

Step 2: Half a dozen times a year (not necessarily on any kind of schedule) pull out the card, read it through twice, and jot down the five biggest problems from this list (following) that you think will face you over the next few years. (This is a good airport activity, between flights.)

Systems—accounting and controls
Running out of money
Space, machinery, and equipment
Market acceptance of our products or services
Staying up with the competition—or ahead
Being in the right markets, getting out of poor ones
Keeping enough trained people on all levels
Coping with regulation and public opinion

*Spreading myself too thin, getting some depth and
continuity so that I can take a vacation
Getting fresh ideas
Personal, family, estate*

Step 3: Now jot down beside the five problems you chose from the list just given the date by which it will be absolutely necessary that you have a workable solution *implemented.*

Step 4: Now estimate how long it will take you to come up with a workable solution for each of these. Choose such time periods as

    a. less than a year
    b. about a year
    c. probably a couple of years
    d. more than three years

Step 5: Now go to your secretary with the list of problems from step 2, the must-have-it-done dates of step 3, and the how-long-it'll-take-us guesses of step 4, and ask your secretary to type you up a list like this:

    a. which problems you need to be working on today
    b. which problems you can wait a year to work on
    c. which problems you can wait two or more years to work on
    d. which problems you can forget about for now

Step 6: Ask your secretary to keep this list and to add to it problems and timetables you will give her (or him) from time to time. Also ask your secretary to remind you with a written note each time a problem gets into the 5a category (things to be working on today) or that stays there longer than six months with no visible progress.

Step 7: Each time you complete action on one of the problems in step 2 tell your secretary to take it off the list and reward yourself. (I mean it, something good! The world works on incentives, and you deserve to collect.)

Step 8: If other people will be involved in solving the problems in step 2, make certain each of them knows

a. what he or she is responsible for doing
b. when you expect the job to be finished
c. what is the next date you want to meet with him or her

Ask your secretary to remind you and the other parties at least two working days in advance of each meeting date. When the other people have performed their part, if they've done a good job, reward them.

I Love It, Coach,
But I Still Ain't Got Time

I don't believe you. But if you don't have the time, and if your secretary *can* do all those things in steps 1 through 8, give him or her a raise and a title, sit back, and let your ex-secretary tell you what to do. You just got yourself a planning staff!

Notes

1. *The Wall Street Journal,* September 11, 1979, pp. 1, 34.
2. List adapted from George Steiner, *Top Management Planning* (New York: Macmillan, 1969), pp. 112-113.

FOUR

Operational Considerations In Long-Range Planning

How can you make all these
nutty ideas work after you've
memorized the book?

The two leading recipes for success are building a better mousetrap and finding a bigger loophole.

Edgar A. Shoaff

This chapter is about operational considerations in long-range planning; that is, can we make these nutty ideas work? We begin with . . .

APPROPRIATE TIME HORIZONS; WHAT IS LONG RANGE? OR OLD DRUNKS NEED TO PLAN TOO

My mother Minerva Levin used to tell the story about an old drunk named Sam who attended a Southern revival meeting where a hellfire and brimstone preacher prophesied the end of the world in 40,000 years. Being a little hard of hearing, Sam leaned over to the person next to him and asked, "How many years did he say?" "Forty thousand," said the neighbor. "Thank God," said Sam, "I thought I heard him say four thousand." My mother loved it. I never realized until much later what an insightful view of excessively long planning horizons it contains.

Just Show Me the One That Hurts

The July 12, 1979 London *Daily Telegraph* carried an article entitled "Vaccine May End Tooth Decay Forever." That grabbed me. The report said a vaccine developed by dental researchers if given to children at ages 5 and 9 might eliminate tooth decay for life. The vaccine had been tried on a colony of monkeys with startling success, but the developers of the vaccine said that it could be months or years before it was ready for testing on human beings.

74

As someone interested in appropriate reactions to environmental events, I began to speculate. What should be the reaction of the 78 deans of dental schools in the United States? Should all practicing dentists apply now for government support for retraining as computer analysts? After all, here is a development that if successful could eliminate virtually all dental caries, thereby rendering obsolete fillings, crowns, and other restorative dentistry. My last thought was how thousands of dentists might look lined up in front of welfare offices twiddling their mirrors and picks.

Alarmist, I said to myself. Did penicillin produce mass unemployment among physicians? Do dentists spend 100 percent of their time filling teeth? (It's interesting what childhood memories of the dentist conjure up—he spent 100 percent of *my* time filling teeth.) Does the Food and Drug Administration let new vaccines out for general use overnight? And, last of all, how many months did I have to wait this year to see Doug Strickland, professor of restorative dentistry at the university, who has suffered (profitably) with my mouth for 25 years? Keep it in perspective, I told myself. Penicillin did *not* throw physicians out of work. The Food and Drug Administration has taken 15 years to evaluate chymopapaine enzyme treatment for spinal disc disorder (in place of surgery known as a laminectomy) and still has not released it. And, checking my calendar, I saw that my August 22 appointment with Doug was made late in April.

Diffusion of new technologies can be painfully slow, particularly those in highly regulated areas. Further, we should not forget that the chances of success of the new vaccine are not 100 percent. (People are still working on perpetual motion machines, though in fairness we should note that someone *has* pedaled an airplane across the English Channel.) If we give the vaccine a 50 percent chance of success in the next five years, allowing for testing, controversy, and other delays, and then, if we tack on another five years for FDA approval, we have a ten-year horizon. If we couple that horizon with the fact that restorative dentistry by the profession and by those who teach the profession involves only about one-third of their total professional activity, and if we add the fact that most dentists probably hate working on kids anyhow and the further fact that they are too busy anyhow—it all adds up to enough time to do a nice managerial adjustment. *If* they all keep calm and knock off writing their congressmen and the dental lobby!

My oracle says dental schools would, in time, spend less time training restorative dentists and more time teaching peridontal disease recognition and control. Those in restorative dentistry would still have their hands full, what with teeth broken off biting hard candy, kicked out in soccer matches, ground down by jaw clenching, or requiring cosmetic perfection for modeling and TV careers. There would be plenty of the usual work to do and plenty of time to switch gradually into other treatments of mouth disorders. So I doubt Ray White, dean of the dental school here, will be calling me anytime soon about the impact of startling new technologies on the School of Dentistry's planning horizon. (And let it come soon, I say, if it will get rid of the screaming kids and let me in two months earlier to see Doug.)

Close Calls, Close Horizons

My good friend Claude, of Greensboro, North Carolina, is a "reviver of sick dogs" and a master at his profession. He snatches moribund companies from the jaws of death and revives them faster and with better long-term prospects of a cure than anyone I know—*anyone*. His record is phenomenal; so is his income, naturally.

Claude comes in, looks at your wreck, makes a quick assessment of its chances, lays out for you how much of the stock he wants if he saves it, and that's it. The rest is sheer poetry. I take a day off with Claude sometimes when he's between "revivals"; we fly somewhere for a good meal or a golf match, or sometimes just to talk as good friends should. He tells me how far ahead a miracle worker plans when he's laying the hands on a very sick company. It's variable, Claude says. "When I'm first called in, I make a quick assessment as to whether it can last thirty days." Claude claims—and you can't argue with success—that in 30 days you can work wonders with current assets and miracles with neophyte bank officers, if you're mean enough. "If I think it can last thirty days I know my chances of saving it go immediately to 50 percent. If that's the case, then I think in terms of one year, because I don't want to stay anywhere more than a year. I try to figure out the chances of it being alive one year hence and what it would be worth then. If the chances are better than 75 percent, and if I can get an agreement today for my share of the projected worth at that time, I'll do a deal."

Claude is a George Allen planner, heart and soul. Defining winning as staying alive, he wants a winning season *this* year and the hell with the future till it gets here. George Allen, as we know, was criticized loudly for mortgaging the future of the Redskins by trading away young blood in the draft for skilled old men of the game. Claude, like George, knows he's mortgaging the future of the company every time he fires a loyal employee, antagonizes a banker, threatens a customer with an overdue account receivable, and drops research on a promising product to generate money for the payroll Friday. The future isn't the point, he tells me. "My strategic objective is to survive, and to survive you mortgage the future. My profession is reviving the dead with heroic measures and meanness, and if I can just keep them going 365 days I'll give a 50-year mortgage to anybody who'll take it. If I go beyond a year I begin to let too many people-organizational-happiness-attitude considerations get in the way of my saving this company." Claude's right. Going to the poorhouse holding hands and singing is still going to the poorhouse.

Now you've heard the long and short of planning horizons, but let me just tell you one about the *long* view (so long you can't see that far).

Three-Digit Planning Horizons

If your name were Methuselah, a planning horizon of 100 years wouldn't make you blush, but finding a three-digit horizon in this day and time is rough. The standard folklore here directs us to consider the Douglas fir industry out in the Pacific Northwest. Forestry experts say that you can grow a Douglas fir big enough to cut for pulpwood in about 100 years or so. Large paper companies dependent on Douglas fir trees for their raw material need the same output from their long-range planning process as everyone else—that is, they need to know whether to plant seedlings this afternoon. (OK, so they skip a couple of days, and no one in 2080 would know the difference. Don't nitpick.)

If long-range planning can't say something about appropriate behavior for *today*, it hasn't said much at all. One important outcome of the long-range planning process in the Northwest pulp and paper companies is the answer to this question: "Should we plant trees today, Coach?" Here again the vagaries of 100-year planning horizons are mitigated a bit by our environment. (It giveth and it taketh away.) First, if we do plant trees, and we do see the market for pulpwood disappearing before our eyes in only 40 years, we could sell off the entire forest at that time. Heaven forbid, you say, the loss would be staggering. True, but what's the present value of that loss discounted at any realistic rate? Aha, you say, saved by mathematics again! Well, there is more to it than that. Forestry schools are experimenting with all kinds of accelerating agents that, if successful, might reduce the growing time to something nearer 80 years. Big deal, you say, that's worse than your mother's 40,000-year drunk joke. Well, the best I can do is leave you with this thought: If the paper industry goes belly up during the next 50 years, you can always sell the trees for basic chemicals. (They're actually worth a lot of money as a source.) Isn't there someone who'll take this risk for us, you ask. Probably. Lloyds of London insures daredevil motorcycle riders and supertankers, movie stars' legs, and opera singers' voices. Someone, somewhere will probably insure your market for Douglas fir trees—at a handsome price. After all, it is a handsome risk. (But, remember, the future doesn't come free; the price is risk. Payoff is the return.)

What can we glean in general rules for behavior from these stories?

First, planning horizons are not fixed. This is important. Whoever thought up the first five-year plan did us a disservice, because it is now set in concrete. Whereas 100 years might be appropriate for the specialized problems of the pulp and paper industry, it is meaningless as a time frame for most other organizations. Moral: Tailor the time to the environment—one year to a hundred.

Second (a corollary to the first), more is not necessarily better. In choosing planning horizons, if you look out at the world three years at a time and see everything of consequence for today's behavior in your organization, then spending the time and money to look out six years is foolishness. Use good judgment as to how far out is enough. This is what you're paid for.

Third, it is entirely legitimate for planning horizons to change over time. That, in fact, is a happy outcome of the long-range planning process. After all, it is the rate of change in the environment relative to the business we're in that determines how long we ought to plan for. As we hammered home in Chapter 2, the futurity of *present* decisions is what long-range planning is all about. Therefore, if our long-range planning indicates that the environment is moving faster and faster with respect to our present products or services, it is common sense to *increase* our long-range planning horizon instead of pouring concrete around it at some arbitrarily chosen level. (And five years is still the worst culprit.)

Fourth, different decisions require different time horizons; therefore, time is a function of the type of decision and not vice versa. You should not use the same planning horizon at every level in your organization. If your company has five levels, and if the top and bottom levels both use four-year planning horizons and make asset-committing decisions accordingly, your fifth level is behaving as a constraint to strategy execution, not as a support to it. By definition, time flexibility must increase as we go down the organization, not decrease. If you find your shop foreman doing ten-year planning, chances are he's screwing up today's output.

Fifth, as we go down the organization, it's legitimate, even desirable, that the long-range planning process become less entrepreneurial and more extrapolative. Whereas it is certain disaster for the top management of a company to consider its planning environment as static, it is generally profitable for lower-level managers to assume that their world will remain fairly well fixed over the near term. To assume otherwise would have the entire organization running around wondering what they should be doing, when everyone knows that this state of confusion is reserved solely for top management.

OK, at this point we know a little about the time period to plan for. Now let's consider the angle of attack—on the outside, on the inside, up, down, where do we grapple with this thing?

INSIDE–OUT VERSUS OUTSIDE–IN
PLANNING: SHOULD WE LOOK AT
US OR THEM? OR, POGO, JIM,
AND SATCHEL PAIGE ON
INSIDE–OUT PLANNING

Pogo said, "We has met the enemy and he is us." That translates roughly into long-range planning parlance as follows: "Internal shortcomings particular to this organization prevent it from recognizing and exploiting the manifold economic opportunities available in the current environment." (Pogo said it better.) These shortcomings of course could include lack of a good planning system, inability to forecast even modestly well, no execution or follow-through abilities, or a dozen other maladies. In any event, it clearly defines the problems as internal, not environmental.

My good friend Jim is president of a very successful miniconglomerate in the communications industry in Chapel Hill. Jim says the measure of an organization's success is its "humpability factor." (And I've never seen an organization the size of his—250 persons—in my experience with more humpability than Jim's.) Humpability is Jim's term for sheer work, output, effort, push, drive—Jim says once he established absolute, unflagging humpability in his organization, the firm found that it could do anything better than the competition. (It's a fact. His company is in eight separate businesses, and all do well.) Jim's focus is on the inside—keeping up the humpability of the troops. "Whatever comes through the door, we can probably make money at it," he says. He probably can; the financial health of his diverse holdings attests to it.

Satchel Paige would have liked Jim. Satchel's famous dictum is "Don't look back, someone may be gainin' on you." That is, do your best, don't worry about the "outside"; if you're good enough, the inside will take care of the outside. Well, Satchel Paige kept pitching baseball into his fifties, oblivious to the environmentally demonstrable fact that baseball players reach their prime by 29 and for all intents and purposes are obsolete by 35. Satchel Paige had both wisdom and humpability.

Where everybody is doing roughly the same thing, that's where humpability counts. And that's an inside–out planning situation. Can we do it better? Sure we can; here's how. And the plan unfolds—from the inside out.

Sid and Buddy on Outside-In
Planning

Sid and Buddy are my two friends in the corrugated box business. Now, in all the world, there is no more competitive business than this one (in spite of what I said about Seventh Avenue and my wife's cousin Mike in the knock-off business).

Sid first. He used to have what they call a setup box plant, where he made all those nice, shiny paper-covered boxes you used to buy gowns and hosiery in. With the advent of sales on hangers for expensive gowns and of folding boxes for hosiery, Sid had to look around (to put it mildly) for something else to do. Now he owns what's called in the corrugated trade a sheet plant. Because he didn't want to invest the millions it takes to buy a corrugating machine, he buys the finished corrugated sheets from his competitors, the big paper companies, then proceeds to make the sheets into boxes on a very inexpensive secondhand printer-slotter. Then he sells the boxes in direct competition with the big boys. Why, you say, do the big corrugated companies sell sheets to him and keep him in business in the first place? Good question. Sid's long-range planning resulted in what you could call a niche strategy. He looked around—outside—very carefully. He saw that the big paper box companies were beating themselves bloody in the market. No place for a mouse in an elephant camp said Sid. Wait a minute, though, what does the ground look like under a herd of elephants (O.K., so it's only four elephants). Like this . . .

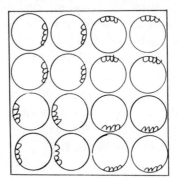

"Ah," says Sid, "if I try a 'little elephant' strategy (⌒) , I get stomped (Southern expression for going belly up in business). But if I try a ⟨⟩ strategy, it fits neatly in the holes between the elephant feet." The rest is implementation. Elegant! Sid buys sheet from the big guys and competes only on the orders they don't want, that is, 213 of this special kind of box, 45 of these, 34 to pack sofas in, and so on. The big boys are ecstatic; here is this little guy, relieving them of those cost-ripping, production-line wrenching setups for 213 boxes. He takes their *nuisance* business. Put him out of business? Are you insane? They love Sid. And Sid prospers—a beautiful example of looking outside to see opportunities even in a grossly overcrowded market.

Now Buddy. Buddy is a former student of mine—an excellent one who went to work for one of the big corrugated companies after college, selling boxes. He was so good that he sold too many, made too much money, earned more than the president. You know the deal—he was too good for them to keep. So Buddy quits and looks around for something to do in the box industry. Well, he sees Sid and Sid's friends all around the country running sheet plants, and that seems crowded to him. Actually it looks like this to Buddy:

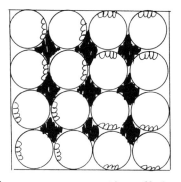

with all the black spaces representing all the sheet plants, like Sid's. "Ah," says Buddy, "disaggregate! Look at the parts, not the whole, to see the light." So Buddy takes a very careful blown-up look at *one* black space, and it looks like this:

"Ah," says Buddy, "if I try a strategy, I get stomped (Southern expression for going belly up in the black space business). But, if I try a ● strategy, it fits in the holes *between* the things that fit in the holes." Once again, a very perspicacious look *outside* to see where the unexploited opportunities lie. So Buddy gets a few coins together, and with about $50,000 of used machinery he begins making all those nasty little bent, die-cut corrugated packing pieces that fit inside corrugated boxes to keep things from breaking in shipment. I don't know what you call it in the trade (except profitable), but let's call it a PP plant (packing-piece plant). Buddy now has *his* profitable niche, a place where the big boys fear to tread (they don't want to get into the PP business), and a place where Sid doesn't want to go at all (he's just got his troops trained to make small runs of special-purpose boxes). Both my friends do quite well as a result of having looked *outside* in their long-range planning process to spot an opportunity. Had they looked inside, Sid would now be bankrupt in the setup box business, and Buddy would still be applying for jobs with a box company willing to employ an overaggressive salesperson (that's what they used to call him) and pay him more than the president. First Moral: Sid and Buddy knew where to look. Second Moral: It takes judgment to know where to look. Third Moral: Buddy did $4 million last year and netted six figures after taxes.

On Getting Inside–Out
and Outside–In Confused

I used to go to Washington once a week to do consulting work for a large suburban public school system there. "Bring them into the computer age," that was my job. At the time, they had two computers and 200,000 students.

One of the first things I did was build one of those fancy forecasting simulator models that, when you feed it data about birth rates, population shifts, school capacities, family mobility, and so forth, spits out forecasts by age of student and family movement for up to ten years into the future—computer-aided outside-in-planning (pretty neat, I thought). Each time we ran it, the message came out clear: the mass movement into this suburban school system characteristic of the 1960s would change in the mid-1970s; there simply would be fewer child-rearing families in the county, particularly in the eastern part of the county.

Now this particular school system was a paragon among public school systems—affluent, well managed, staffed with conscientious planners, a real class act in public school education. The thing they prided themselves on most was that they didn't have one mobile classroom in the entire county. That's right, not one. All their kids went to classes in permanent, expensive, well-built school buildings that the administration put up at the rate of about five a year. Clearly a tribute to good long-range planning.

But the model kept indicating that there would be fewer and fewer kids, that in fact the kids would all but disappear in parts of the county in ten years. Meanwhile all these permanent, well-designed masonry school buildings with 40 year lives, were popping up like mushrooms. Why? Outside–in planning surely dictated that the building program be tailored to long-term demand. From that premise should have flowed the planned construction of less expensive schools designed consciously to have 10- to 15-year lives. No, said the school board, we just don't build those kinds of schools here. Thus, inside–out considerations ("we are not the kind of people who build temporary schools") dominated the realities of the marketplace for education. The inevitable happened. Today there are fewer kids, half-empty schools (some schools closed), and a constant effort to find some productive use for all those school buildings that they don't need. Sometimes it's 25 adults meeting two nights a week studying flower arranging in a $2.6-million building designed for 350 students. Painful—that's what it feels like to confuse outside–in and inside–out.

OK, I've never read a book on long-range planning that didn't argue that managers should look first to the marketplace to decide where their organization ought to be and what it ought to be doing. As you know by now, that's the essence of outside–in planning. It typifies the traditional process: first, find a market; then, see if we're good enough to tap it. Ted Levitt wrote a widely read, highly influential article for *Harvard Business Review* entitled "Marketing Myopia." In it, he attempted to condition thousands of top executives to define their market in the broadest possible sense in the face of inevitable change. Consequently, if you follow Levitt closely, broad market forecasts are the pillars of your strategic planning.

But Levitt's advice needs a grain of salt. Look at the facts. Markets move so rapidly and in such diverse directions today that forecasting the size, or even the direction, of the market isn't as easy as it used to be. Whenever you are sure you know where the market is heading, remind yourself that more and more organizations are developing the capability to serve more and more markets: bowling alley companies make boats, tobacco companies make dog food, and liquor companies sell chicken. Therefore, they *can* and probably *will* see the same opportunities you do—maybe even about the *same time* you do. This sophisticated invasion of new areas you perhaps had staked out for yourself is likely to accelerate over time, not diminish. But . . .

1. Don't panic.
2. Don't stop monitoring your markets.
3. Do, however, keep in mind that markets can be *made* as well as followed.

Astute internal judgement ("feel") can *create* a style, a trend, or a movement. It was foreign automobile makers, not the homegrown market researchers in Detroit, who first weaned Americans off large cars; and style, not energy, was the issue. If everybody does the same thing, the organization that does it most efficiently wins. But if you can do something either much better—or much differently—from everybody else, the possibilities are tremendous. Now let me tell you a couple of stories to illustrate.

My favorite inside–out planning story is about my former student Bob. When Bob was in our MBA program he used to say that when he graduated he wanted to be a painter. The faculty was impressed; they thought that a painter alumnus would lend luster to the business school. What we didn't realize was that Bob meant buildings, not canvases. We were shocked. Why would a bright young man with an MBA want to go into an overcrowded, dirty business like commercial painting? He started work after graduation as foreman for a painting contractor down in eastern North Carolina. Within a year he was the contractor's superintendent. Family and salary considerations then led Bob to quit and open his own painting contracting firm. (At this point, note again how not paying top people top money is one of the great incentives to new enterprise development.) Bob chose Charlotte, North Carolina, a particularly overcrowded market, we astute faculty members remarked. But here's what Bob knew. Reliability among painters is like honor among thieves. He knew the agonies owners and general contractors went through dealing with painting subcontractors operating out of pickup trucks with no records, no schedule, no business manner. Enter Bob in three-piece suit. He rents a nice office, prints up a four-color brochure, and talks like the MBA he is. *Mirabile dictu!* A painting contractor dressed like a banker. More: A painter who actually returns phone calls, keeps business hours, and shows up when he says he will—sober yet. Within four years Bob was a force in the local market; today he does over 3 million volume, nets six figures and is worth more than anyone in his MBA class (except maybe Bill, more about whom later). Quick and dirty analysis: Bob delivers the same service as 875 other painters within 200 miles of Charlotte but so much better that he has a completely differentiated service from the rest. He is the *only* painter who can do what he does. Now what's that if not the epitome of inside–out long-range planning? Bob has a lot of humpability too.

My favorite outside–in success story is about condoms. Heaven knows how many retail outlets exist for this product— millions probably. Every drugstore in the world sells them; every other gas station men's room has a condom machine. The market for condoms is known, forecastable with unerring accuracy, and exploited by larger companies. Traditional outside–in long-range planning would have suggested that getting into the condom business as a new venture should be number 16 on a list of three financially attractive fliers. But the people at Adam and Eve in Chapel Hill know what they're about. They found a niche. Several years ago they started a business that distributes condoms nationwide by mail order. They buy condoms, receive condoms, advertise condoms, unwrap condoms, rewrap condoms, ship condoms, and make money on condoms like you wouldn't believe. (*Would* you believe $5 million annual sales?)

Now probably 90 percent of our population—say, 200 million Americans—live within a ten–minute drive of a retailer of this product. So who buys by mail when you can get it around the corner? (1) Anybody who wants anonymity. (2) Anybody who wants a slightly jazzier version of the standard product. For the sexually adventurous, Adam and Eve puts out a catalog illustrating the 59 varieties of condoms you won't find in the drugstore even if you aren't too shy to ask. And, if you *are* too shy, join the anonymous throng of mail-order purchasers, ranging from adolescent boys in small towns, to women who like to keep a spare contraceptive method on hand, to adult men who just can't look somebody in the eye and ask for a packet of Trojans, to college fraternities ordering en masse, to— (probably) your respectable next-door neighbor. In other words, almost everybody. Who would have believed it?

CENTRALIZED VERSUS
DECENTRALIZED
LONG-RANGE PLANNING,
OR WHERE SHOULD YOU DO IT?

I've worked with some people who own and operate a very successful chain of retail jewelry stores, about 100 in number. They take great pride in telling everybody that their store managers have "nearly absolute autonomy" in planning and running their operation. That is, the managers can do anything they think is profitable; as long as this turns out to be true, the autonomy (and the store manager's job) continues.

If we take this statement literally, this must be an extreme example of highly decentralized long-range planning, that is, 100 individuals, each setting his or her goals in lieu of top management of the company setting goals to be carried out at store level. Here's how it really works. One of the first things that strikes you in their stores is the computer terminal. (Each store has one; they're all connected to the main computer at corporate headquarters.) In an interview, the store manager says that he is free to order and sell "anything." Translation: Anything that was approved in his annual merchandise plan and conditioned upon his being "open to buy" (that is, with some capital left in his budget for inventory). Furthermore, he cannot add credit sales unless his accounts receivable allocation is not used up (he must collect a dollar, so to speak, before he can charge another dollar). Most of the stores are in shopping malls (a location decision the store manager didn't make). And all ordering at the store level is done through a central buying and distribution arrangement. Oh yes, and pricing decisions are made by the corporate office.

OK, you already figured it out! The long-range planning in this company is hardly decentralized. The important decisions are all planned at headquarters: what business they will be in, the most appropriate location for each physical facility, the appropriate asset investment at each location, the pricing structure, the physical distribution system, and even the annual merchandising plan. The store manager has local planning authority over lines to carry and feature, credit-granting authority, and management of store personnel (subject, of course, to company personnel policies)—all of which is closely monitored daily with a computer.

This setup is no aberration among planning models. In fact, it's a fairly standard long-range planning model for retailing. The major strategic decisions are made where they must be made in any successful organization, *at the top*. In that sense, strategic long-range planning *is* highly centralized (where it belongs). Planning for operations at the store level is highly decentralized, (where it belongs), and tightly controlled. (The latter is a matter of management style and not subject to broad generalizations about what works and what doesn't.) So, in fact, planning in the general sense of that word is done at two locations, but strategic long-range planning is done exclusively at the top.

Meet Anne,
Our Company Planner

The jewelry chain has two levels of planning—one strategic, the other operational. In many companies, it's common to have eight, sometimes ten, levels of long-range planning, each level doing its thing to operationalize company strategy. And all ten levels can legitimately be doing long-range planning (with different time horizons, of course). But only one of them decides what business they ought to be in. That's the critical difference.

So you walk in the door of this $50 million company and someone says, "Meet Anne, our company planner." Heaven help us if Anne (and only Anne) does all the planning an organization this size needs! But, if she gathers and disseminates information as a basis for planning, if she provides staff planning help to other parts of the organization, if she coordinates plans from various departments, and if she works as a resource to the top management of the company as they formulate strategic long-range plans, then one person *can* do the work. Let's say it one more time this way: (1) it's *good* when everybody does some planning in an organization; (2) it's *bad* when everybody (or nobody) does strategic long-range planning in an organization; (3) it's *bad* when one person tries to do all the planning in an organization; (4) it's *good* when one person coordinates the planning functions in an organization; (5) it's *great* when all this works; (6) it *helps* to have lots of humpability!

Yeah, Coach,
But I Know
This Conglomerate

It used to be fashionable to talk of highly diversified organizations with highly decentralized planning systems—a group of enlightened, modern-day entrepreneurs held together with only the tiniest gossamer threat of encouragement from the top. U.S. Industries in the 1969s was a premier organization of the type, a corporation made up of previously very highly successful individual companies, all run by their original owners. They followed a kind of "do your own thing, but don't forget to send money" strategy. The reasoning went that, after all, if these fearless entrepreneurs had done their own thing successfully, there was no inherent reason why this degree of profitable autonomy could not continue under the corporate umbrella in a decentralized manner with liberty, justice, and the advantages of public stock for all. Well, they didn't make it to the moon. The same decentralized creative greed that set individually successful strategies for 20 or so independent companies did not seem able to make it work for one corporation. Financial synergy was the very essence of the conglomerate's plan, but how to achieve it went virtually unplanned. After a while, when the fault became obvious, the corporation tightened up strategic planning. But centralized strategic planning is not loved by all. Who gets the money to invest tends to be the bitchiest question in these sort of organizations. (Just poll the have's and have-not's around capital budgeting time for their views on centralized strategic planning.)

In this instance, strategic planning tended to corral some of the previously successful cowboy capitalism, controls replaced some of the autonomy, and some of the spark simply went out. It took years to get the whole deal back on track. No, Virginia, you really can't decentralize strategic long-range planning successfully. Someone must always decide for everyone in the organization what we *could* be, what we *ought* to be, and what we *should* be doing if we don't like what we are today.

BUT WHAT IF MY HORSE
GIVES OUT IN MIDSTREAM?

Coca-Cola is high up on everybody's list of perennially successful American companies. By the 1950s it had nearly a thousand bottlers putting out the magic elixir. ("Dope," they used to call it in the South—"going to have me a dope," the old folks would say.) Anyhow, in the good old simple days, packaging was mostly one size bottle, 6 ounces.

Some of the bottlers were owned by Coca-Cola, some by fairly large, well-run corporations, but most of the bottlers had been in families for years . . . and years . . . and years. A Coke franchise was looked upon in most circles as a guaranteed gold mine. Hell, those machines practically ran themselves: syrup in, money out. It was great. And Coca-Cola's corporate strategy was to let the bottlers do anything they wanted as long as they bought the syrup and sold lots of Coke. The years went by, the money rolled in, and some of the families failed to pay attention to organizational development, position strength, financial controls, physical distribution logistics—all the niceties of making money. And the years went by some more, and untrained sons of untrained sons inherited Coca-Cola bottling franchises.

Then came the 1960s: multiple packages, complex distribution and production planning, and, worse, fierce competition. Coke felt the sting of being number 2 in some markets.

Let's get this thing going, they thought. If we tell the bottlers what to do, they'll do it. But lots of the untrained sons couldn't do physical distribution planning, and they didn't understand the need for financial planning, and they couldn't master production planning when you had 50 different packages and sizes, and so on and so on.

Coca-Cola responded by changing a previously un-beatable strategy. Instead of leaving bottlers to their own devices, they now promoted mergers and acquisitions of the smaller, less efficient bottlers by the larger, more capable, often corporately managed bottlers. In other words, they got their distribution organization into the hands of people who could implement a competitive marketing strategy at the bot-tler level. By the late 1960s there were about half as many bot-tlers as there had been in the simple old days. And now there are even fewer. Moral: Doctrinaire views about anything are generally wrong over time. So if someone tells you you can't switch horses in midstream, tell him to hush and hold your horse for you, and then ease over *very* carefully. It *can* be done—and so can changing the degree of (appropriate) plan-ning centralization. Very carefully. (In the interests of sym-metry, which I urged on you in Chapter 3, I'm bound to report that Scripto, Inc., the Atlanta-based pen, pencil, and lighter maker, changed corporate strategies and top management about ten times in 30 years, and what did it get them? Stomped (you know, a Southern expression . . .).

FROM THE HORIZONTAL
TO THE VERTICAL,
TOP–DOWN OR
BOTTOM–UP, COACH?

My university sets a terrible example of bottom–up long-range planning. At Chapel Hill we're comprised of 14 colleges and schools, enrolling 21,000 students. Periodically, the chancellor puts out a memo to the vice chancellors and provost calling for a long-range plan, and the vice chancellors and provost put out a memo to all the schools and colleges calling for a long-range plan, and the deans of the schools and colleges put out a memo to all the department heads calling for a long-range plan, and the department heads put out a memo to their faculties calling for a long-range plan. Then the faculty members send their long-range plan to their department heads, and the department heads edit, condense, and retype the plans, put them into a common binder, and send them to their deans who edit, condense, and retype all the department plans, put them into a common binder, and send them to the vice chancellors or provost, who edit, condense, and retype them, put them into a common binder, and send them to the chancellor's planning assistant who edits, retypes, and condenses them and adds a bit of editorial glue before putting them in a common binder and giving them to the chancellor. End of tale. End of plan too.

This bottom–up planning process results in a nicely bound, 500-page document consisting of an expensively edited set of "look what a good job we're doing these days, send more money and we'll do even better" stories without a common thread linking them, much less a strategic thought. As long as this document is used to placate the legislature, the trustees, the big donors, and the general public, we're not in trouble. But heaven help us if we ever try to use one of these plans for its ostensible purpose, the making of strategic choices for the university. Armageddon!

A *bona fide*, strategic, long-range plan for the University of North Carolina at Chapel Hill would set out to define what we ought to become over the next 10 to 20 years, given the world in which we live, teach, are funded, and do research. Instead, the long-range planning process we follow results in a collection of short-run plans, each done by a separate part of the university to defend or expand its turf. (Planning horizons in the last plan ranged from 3 to 25 years.)

Now everybody in the university knows that the real long-range planning process is a political one that starts with your trying to get the trustees to approve a new degree program that your department absolutely must have (look at the hundreds of students who have petitioned you for this curriculum—and they're the bottom of the bottom-up theory, right?). Then, if you get it, bargaining with the provost for X new positions to staff the new curriculum; then, when the new faculty outgrows your present facilities, bargaining some more with everybody you know in the North Carolina General Assembly and the advisory budget commission to get the money to build the new building to house the new faculty to teach the new students and it does go on and on.

You might pounce on me with the claim that this is just Quinn's "logical incrementalism" at work from Chapter 2, but I don't buy that and you know it. In this instance, the whole elaborate long-range planning process is nothing but jumping through hoops while waving a paper with dollar signs on it. There's no long-range plan when the "plan" fails to illuminate and select strategic alternatives for the organization. That's so basic and so important that I'll say it again. It's not a plan if it doesn't illuminate and choose strategic alternatives for the organization.

Top-Down Planning

One of the newer deans at the university did not subscribe to the bottom-up long-range planning process just outlined. And he said as much at a prestigious academic gathering where he unveiled *his* "Top-Down Planning For A School" approach. This occurred just a few months into his tenure.

Now virtually all faculty members have a strong streak of individualism. Some also have a high need to "feel involved," regardless of whether they have an opinion and want to add input or not. A key to successful academic administration is letting everyone "feel involved"—the old-fashioned expression for which is listening—whether those involved have anything to say or not. A smaller academic constituency is comprised of the movers and shakers of a department or school, those who insist that strategy formulation is the sole province of the faculty, not the administration, and who often get their way. This constituency needs to set strategy, then leave the dean to find the money to implement it.

In this instance, the new dean's publicly articulated top–down approach antagonized both segments of his constituency, those who wanted to be listened to and those who didn't care who listened as long as they got to make the plan. Upshot: The dean got stomped (Southern expression for "after serious reflection, returns to full-time teaching and research").

The Best of Both

In its "pure" form, bottom–up planning is a bust. It lacks the strategic overview required to plan for the organization as a whole. It is fragmented. It suffers from an extrapolative approach at operating levels—doing more of what we're doing now, as a result of insulation from the larger world outside. Bottom-up planning also is prone to abrupt strategy changes at the operating levels, levels that think they're so far down that nobody at the top will notice if they chuck out the old plan and make up something new. ("Hey, you all, let's use all this leftover plastic—yeah, let's make frisbees! Market them by mail. Great idea!")

But it's got its good points. (Symmetry, remember?) A bottom–up planning approach works reasonably well in very small organizations kind of like a government by committee of the whole. You just have to have a small enough whole. Furthermore, bottom–up planning is satisfactory in situations calling for extrapolative extensions of current strategy—moving on out the same strategic line. Best of all, bottom–up planning generates ownership. People get involved. You may want to give bottom–up planning a whirl; if so, avoid these pitfalls: (1) a complex planning process with endless committee meetings strung out over too long a time with too many compromises required for consensus—you'll frustrate people who spend a lot of their personal time only to see their ideas traded off in the end "for the good of the whole organization"—better never to have owned an idea at all than to have owned and sacrificed a pet notion; (2) a complex or rapidly changing environment where heroic strategic departures may be required—too high a risk here that predictably conservative consensus-type plans aren't the medicine you need—and you might get stomped (with a smile on everyone's face, however).

Now for the good news. Top–down planning in its "pure" form is a bust too. Planning should *begin* at the top, but isolating it there is bad administrative style and terrible planning dogma. So, in the best of all possible planning worlds, top management would

1. provide the underlying assumptions on which planning is to be based: who we are, who we want to be, what is the nature of the environment as we see it?

2. seek inputs from all levels of the organization: how tough are we?; do you agree with the nature of the environment as we see it?

3. illuminate strategic alternatives as a framework of possibilities, then ask all levels how do our strengths fit; how do our needs fit; will these ideas work?

4. select a strategy;

5. work hard to get commitment to and ownership of the selected strategy at all levels.

This is the ideal: the top is where the planning begins and ends, but the process is back and forth all the way. This is the pitfall: the entire planning process is localized at the top; interesting dysfunctional reactions ensue (remember the Shah of Iran, the French Revolution, and Brown versus the Board of Education).

"And here's Dick bringing you a recap of today's planning directions."

1. *Inside-out:* Use it when you want to do what other people are already doing, but when you want to knock their socks off doing it better.

   Key question: How can you do it better; what's your competitive advantage?

2. *Outside-in:* Use it when you want to claim some turf, a spot in the market nobody's occupying, a space for a new product, style, or trend.

   Key question: Where's the spot in the environment that you can claim? What can you add to the environment that's not already there?

3. *Top-down and Bottom-up:* Combine all ingredients, mix well. Impetus, basic premises, and most interpretation of data take place at the top. Data generation, some interpretation, suggestions, support come from all along the line, bottom to top. You can't make everybody happy, but don't forget ownership.

"And now for the weather."

CHECK LIST: SIX WAYS TO TELL
WHEN YOU'VE GOT THE RIGHT
PLAN

Check One: Is It Consistent with the Environment?[1] No, we're not endorsing outside-in planning again. We're merely noting that one mark of a successful long-range plan is that it be tuned to the market and to the larger world. It can also, like Bob's painting company, be *based* on a unique competency within ourselves (inside-out approach). But whatever we offer, it must be appropriate to our environment or it won't sell. (Salmon only swim upstream for sex, not for money!)

Check Two: Is the Plan Internally Consistent? Are the parts of the strategy consistent with each other? (I was once asked to help devise a strategy for a family business that would let them (1) grow rapidly, (2) make money, (3) finance it all internally, (4) go public, (5) get rich, and (6) retain control. These six substrategies do not cohabitate as a rule; roped together, they are an inconsistent strategy. A lovely fantasy, though.) Two other questions illuminate consistency within. Are all of us in this organization moving in roughly the same direction? What would happen if all our objectives were fulfilled? (A neat question, remember it—if all your wishes came true, what would actually happen?)

Check Three: Is Our Strategy Appropriate to Our Resources? Here's where it's productive to knock off admiring the inherent magnificence of the strategy itself and question whether we're biting off more than we can chew. Can we afford to implement the strategy? (I met one of my former MBA students in an airport recently. He told me that he'd been phenomenally successful after graduation, starting a wholesale steel business from scratch and building it up to a million dollars a month in sales. How's it doing, I asked? Oh, he said, I grew so fast I ran out of money!) Start with a maximum sustainable growth rate calculation such as that in Chapter 3. Follow that with a body-by-body assessment of the troops you have with you now. If you pass muster on these two, you can pretty much beg, borrow, and steal the rest.

Check Four: Is the Risk in This Strategy the Appropriate Risk? Are we taking on more risk than this organization can afford to handle? Is lower risk–lower reward a better alternative? Are we playing in the right league to suit our personal preferences? Is the risk high enough to be stimulating but not so high as to drive us crazy and ruin our health? (Remember that some poker players love to play 10- to 25-cent poker and play it exceedingly well, but they won't get into a higher stakes game. It is *not* the game of poker that they reject; they have wisely chosen the risk level appropriate to them within the game.)

99

Check Five: Does the Strategy Have an Appropriate Time Horizon? Here we're checking time, environment, and strategy for fit. Have we focused on changes in our unique environment to give ourselves adequate lead time for appropriate response? Are we playing in an eight-year game with a five-year strategic plan? Conversely, are we playing in a five-year response game but pestering our management with environmental signals eight years away that have no bearing on the current plan? Would anybody be justified in calling us George Allen planners? That is, are we mortgaging the future too heavily in order to look good now, with consequences that will not be evident for some time to come?

Check Six: Is the Strategy Workable? Bottom line: Is it working? If we wait till some future date to see, it may be too late. But if we can't bottom line it, we can at least check our pro forma with three criteria. (1) Is it *technically* workable—can we make them and sell them? (2) Is it *economically* workable—if we can make them and sell them, do the numbers work out? (3) Is it *operationally* workable—will the organization *let* it work? Do people here believe in it, will they support its implementation?

Hut-One,
Hut-Two,
Hike

If the checks all work out to yes, congratulations. Your chances of success have just gone up. (I gave you credit for humpability to start with.) What next, Coach? Well, you pick up that plan now and run like hell. But don't look back; you might get stomped (you remember, a Southern expression . . .).

NOTES

[1]Adapted from Seymour Tilles, "How to Evaluate Corporate Strategy, "*Harvard Business Review.* (Vol. 41: No. 4) 1963, pp. 111–121.

FIVE

Behavioral Considerations In Long-Range Planning

Putting the "touchy-feely" stuff
in the long-range plan.

A round man cannot be expected to fit in a
square hole right away. He must have time
to modify his shape.

Mark Twain

LONG-RANGE PLANNING,
PERCEIVED REWARDS
AND PUNISHMENTS, OR
WATCH OUT FOR THE RATS

All of us still behave in some ways exactly as we did in high school. In math it was important to find out what the teacher stressed on quizzes—definitions or problem solution. If the teacher was a definition type, rote memory was the right response—you stuffed yourself full of anticipated answers and tried to hold on to them until you could regurgitate on paper. If he or she stressed solving problems, watch out; you really had to know something about math to pass. Worst of all, though, if the teacher was one of that notorious breed who didn't give quiz problems like those in the book, but rather his or her own brainbusters, it was pure hell because then you actually had to *understand* mathematical reasoning, not just remember how to solve the problems in the book. We can characterize this pattern as behaving for the report card. And we may have gotten smoother in our approach to it over the years, but may lightning strike our lying tongues if we claim to have stopped behaving for the report card when we got too old for report cards anymore. *Plus ca change, plus c'est la même chose.* At 18 we get a report card, at 35 an annual performance review.

Now all the studies we know about support the notion that people behave to fill their needs and that, in doing so, they examine the rewards and penalties built into the system to find out (1) what gets first prize and (2) what gets last prize. When I was in the ninth grade, I was a real hell raiser. (That was the year before my parents gave up and shipped me off to Oak Ridge Military Institute for "the cure.") My principal, Dave Hicks, would tolerate a lot of things—skipping school, smoking in the boys' room, turning off the master electrical switch; all of these were frowned on, but he wouldn't get on your case too badly for them. (He also rewarded some things too: making grades high enough to get into Beta Club was a guaranteed winner with Dave, as was wearing shoes to school after May 1.) But just you try to bother the new practice teachers—girls not too much older than we were, enduring the trial by fire of practice teaching as part of their senior year at the local teachers' college—just harass one of them and Mr. Hicks would galvanize into action. All he had to hear was that Dick Levin, Dan Bowen, Tom Brandon, and Charles Siceloff had run one of those dedicated young ladies out of the classroom in tears and screaming (our favorite way was to let loose half a dozen rats during class), and retribution was swift and certain. Down the stairs, into his office, down with our pants, and blistered fannies. Justice. It was like the Old Testament. Now that I think back on the consequences, it must have been a really dull day that we resorted to picking on the poor practice teachers.

Military school had its own penalties and rewards. In the first ten minutes I spent there, I learned the hard way that you didn't tell a six-foot two-inch upperclassman to go straight to hell when he told you to shine his shoes. In the next week I learned that if I volunteered to play the piano for Sunday night vesper services, Major Larkins, the commandant, would provide some positive strokes in the form of knocking off a well-deserved demerit or two. And at the end of the first month I found out that Captain Weaver, the math instructor, gave all brainbusters on his quizzes. Oh hell.

Growing up doesn't change us much. We still tend to run toward behaviors that bring us rewards (positive strokes) and away from those that bring us punishments (negative strokes).

And the behavior of sophisticated individuals in a formal organization going through the long-range planning process is only a special case of the general rule.

What Gets Counted Here

Psyching out the organizational climate is every employee's favorite game. With good reason—what gets counted for the report card in this place is a legitimate concern. Appropriate questions which need to be asked (and answered early) include (1) what is the best thing you can do here if you want to get ahead fast, (2) what is the worst thing you can do here if you want to get ahead fast, (3) do they count inputs, (4) do they count outputs, (5) who are the "ins," what are they like, and who are the "outs," and how did they get there? These questions seek to nail down the reward–penalty system of the organization, and each of them has an important bearing on the long-range planning process. Let's get more specific.

If the only variable measured on the organizational report card is your current behavior, the best thing you can do is get on with today's job and finesse planning for tomorrow. If an important variable on the report card is the extent of your planning for tomorrow, then the worst thing you can do is spend too much time on today's job. If the organization counts inputs, then your planning behavior runs to attending all scheduled meetings, meeting all input deadlines, completing all planning forms, and having all your little goals neatly arranged and time-targeted. If the organization counts outputs, then you learn to concentrate on substance, not form—that is, on planning a strategy that will work even at the expense of performing current tasks. If the "ins" are a bunch of good old boys who don't want to rock the boat, then planned strategies tend to be conservative and objectives modest. If the "ins" are tigers, strategic alternatives tend to become more ambitious and exciting and objectives more demanding on the organization. In each instance, the organizational climate influences the kind of long-range planning that is done, the kinds of strategic alternatives that are evaluated, and, consequently, the future of the organization. For this reason, "what gets counted here" is a vital issue.

Do They Think Long or Short Here?

Bosses who "think long" not only measure outputs, they measure them over extended periods of time. On the other hand, bosses who "think short" measure outputs too. But they like them consistent—not necessarily consistently high—and they rarely let you trade off today's output for tomorrow's survival. What does this mean? It's a fact of life that long-range planning takes time, both to do and to implement. If you want lousy ideas, however, we can get them for you this afternoon. Despite the time required for high-quality output, many organizations simply don't permit their managers to take the time to plan effectively. Because the future is relatively easy to mortgage and because most of the liens you put on it by lack of adequate planning are not visible for several years, mortgaging the future is an instinctive executive reaction in organizations, and to bosses, who "think short." George Allen "thought short," and he assumed that the Redskins fans and management also thought short. His only mistake was in "staying long"; 1973 or 1974 would have been a great year for him to have hung it up.

Winston Churchill, on the other hand, understood "thinking long." In speaking of the need to evaluate leadership over a sufficient length of time, he said, ". . . if he trips, he must be sustained. If he makes mistakes, they must be covered. If he sleeps, he must not be wantonly disturbed. If he is no good, he must be pole-axed. But this last extreme process cannot be carried out every day; and certainly not in the days just after he has been chosen."[1]

I love Auguste Rodin's sculpture "The Thinker." Here is a statue of a magnificent-looking man sitting with his head propped on his hand thinking. Just thinking. The posture connotes reflection and concentration. (On the future? Perhaps.) The strongly muscled body connotes power to act even though it is at this moment in repose. To me "The Thinker" exudes the essence of the undisturbed reflection and creativity necessary for successful strategic long-range planning. Now, if your boss came into your office (especially when this week's production in your department was down from last week) and found you with your head in your hands, "thinking"—perhaps even a bit removed from today's company problems (creative corporate dreaming, if you will)—and had to call your name twice to "bring you out," could you rationalize this behavior as long-range planning and get away with it? Is quiet reflection provided for and rewarded by the organization—or are senior executives expected to handle the future simply as a time detail of their present activities? That's the issue here.

When I was 25, I thought short and I didn't understand Rodin. So it was only natural that, when I went into the armed forces, I would think short and not understand Rodin there too. I was a Purchasing and Contracting Officer at Pepperrell Air Force Base, St. Johns, Newfoundland, and I fancied myself a very efficient first lieutenant. Every day, every purchase order got filed, every voucher got posted, every request for proposals was logged out and in, and every possible procurement action had its own checklist designed by me. One day in a fit of pique over why purchasing and contracting had so many problems, Major Willie Lewis, the base supply officer (and a hell of a poker player) said, "Levin, you're a nice kid, what you need to do is stop working and get to work." Willie understood thinking long! (He also ran the Tuesday night poker game at the Officers Club at which every new lieutenant at the base was routinely cleaned out— stomped!) It was some years later before I finally figured out what Willie meant.

MOST OF THIS
NEVER GETS
WRITTEN DOWN

Graduate students in management have a hard time understanding nonverbal communication at other than an intellectual level—you know, the gestures, nuances, and so on that carry real meaning as opposed to the words that just fill up time and space. The behaviors that the organization rewards, the things that get counted, whether people think long or short, and whether they understand Rodin hardly ever gets put down in writing. They become part of the organizational aura, the folklore, what you have to smell rather than see. If you're good at recognizing organizational trail signs, you survive; if you aren't, you get a lot of bruises at work.

My favorite nonverbal communication story took place in the airport in Xian, China. I was safely ensconced in a stall in the men's room (or so I thought) when I heard the door open and several distinctly female voices proceed into the room. In a moment, from the mop and bucket noises they made, I gathered that they were the cleaning crew. They began mopping the floor at the other end of the row of thrones from where I was sitting. As they came mopping up the line, finally one of them stopped directly in front of my stall. She spoke directly to me in Chinese—there simply was no question that she was addressing me. And, although I neither understand nor speak Chinese, I knew exactly what she wanted and complied forthwith! I raised my legs, she mopped "through" and continued down the line. Ah, nonverbal communication. It really works.

BUT CAN'T YOU
SWIM UPSTREAM, COACH?

Wasn't President Kennedy's father a rum runner, and didn't the Nixon presidency produce *some* outstanding administrators, and isn't it true that you *can* fight City Hall (even Tammany was overcome in time, wasn't it?) and don't fanatically reactionary families produce some very liberal offspring, and don't staph germs survive and even thrive in some hospitals? All true, every one of them true. Then why can't a bright, careful, thoughtful, insightful, patient, thorough, wise, politically astute, administratively magnificent long-range-planning-type executive thrive and produce good plans in an environment hostile to planning? He can, she can, but who among us qualifies for that list of adjectives?

True, there *are* exceptions to every rule, especially in behavioral situations. When you're dealing with organizations and feelings, talking in absolutes is dangerous. But the point is still valid that the organizational climate tends to mold and constrain (if not to control) individual outputs over time—even the "best and the brightest" get pressed in the organizational mold. Conclusion: There are a lot of executives who are frightened of "stopping work and getting to work." If you want effective long-range planning, you must provide an organizational climate that encourages, fosters, and rewards effective planning behavior over extended periods of time. That is one of the most significant responsibilities of the chief. The chief can change the climate. And a favorable climate for planning must be created so that this behavior is rewarded. Good planning should be treated as an organizational norm, not as an aberration.

MANAGEMENT STYLES AND
LONG-RANGE PLANNING RESPONSES,
OR, THE BAD GUYS
ALL WEAR BLACK HATS

In the cowboy movies (a teenage Saturday ritual in our small Southern town), it was easy to tell the good guys from the bad guys. Hollywood makes it easy. But organizations don't run on 90-minute schedules; thus, making distinctions between organizational good guys and bad guys is considerably more difficult (but more fun too).

When scholars want to describe how executives behave, they refer to *management style,* and there are as many different taxonomies of management as there are management professors—a horrifying thought. Almost all these competing classification systems avoid talking just about "good guys" and "bad guys." Organizational life is just too complex to reward a two-category behavioral model. (There are still some people who have a simple Theory X and Theory Y view of organizational life, but most are MBA students, and they generally get over it before graduation.) To help us examine the effect on long-range planning of an executive's management style (or for that matter an organization's management style— one does clone off the other in time), we'll use a simple but effective classification system with five different management styles. Voilà, a quick and dirty taxonomy.

1. But Patton Won, Didn't He? George Patton, it was obvious, had a high need for *power*; John D. Rockefeller was similarly constructed. History is full of executives with high power needs. The need is nothing to be ashamed of as long as you work for people who measure outputs not inputs. Power-oriented executives tend to plan "by the numbers" and to set organizational objectives and choose strategic alternatives unilaterally. They are generally not team players. Executives with high power needs never really get good size-up information from the troops below because the troops are justifiably afraid to report weaknesses, especially the real ones. Executives with high power needs don't mind taking high risks, but usually they take them based on their personal risk-taking posture, not on that of the organization they head. This often gets them in a great deal of trouble later. Implementation (laying the plan off on the organization) by power types is generally quite detailed, with everyone's place and target neatly laid out. There is not much room for creative interpretation or deviation from the plan.

The style of long-range planning that results in this instance is somewhat mechanical, has insufficient ownership, and tends toward extrapolative (albeit with high rates of growth sometimes) rather than entrepreneurial strategies. Strategies get forced into implementation even when they should be altered. There is insufficient local adaptation because no one at the implementation level wants to shoot holes in the boss's plan. Feedback about success tends to be warped toward good news (the troops all play Roman messenger—you know, when the Roman messengers brought bad news, the emperor cut off their heads—not much of a participative management style, but you must admit that it sure cuts down on bad news!)

None of this is necessarily bad, and we must not fall victim here to a simplistic bad–good classification scheme. If it works over time, it's good; if it doesn't, it's bad—that's the only test that grownups ought to apply. Power-oriented strategic planning works very well, for example, in emergency situations where consequential decisions must be made under severe time pressures and where organizational commitment is of secondary importance to choosing the right direction for survival.

2. *Groupies Have to Plan Too, You Know.* Some executives (some organizations too), have high *affiliative* needs—they like people, they like being around people, they dislike making people angry, they hate to say no to people, and they spend great amounts of time pleasing people. In organizations headed by these types of executives, long-range planning is highly participative; organizational objectives and risks are identified and chosen through a very deliberate consensus process. The

strategic alternative that results often is a compromise, at a minimum, one that leaves nobody really upset. In general, such a plan does not really tax the maximum strengths of the organization nor does it represent the highest level of risk that could be assumed. The plan is laid off on the organization (implemented) in a highly participative manner, great time and care being taken at every level to get ownership. Individual targets tend to be defined more in general terms than in specifics, with lots of room left for individual interpretation and adaptation. There is a great deal of honest reporting of errors. Performance evaluation is quite loose in these organizations, and good "input style" (trying to do it with a good team attitude) generally excuses bad "output" (screwing up).

An affiliative long-range planning style has its home court advantage too. *If* you have an organization of very bright and totally committed people (a lab full of scientists with humpability, for example) and *if* the environmental rate of change is slow enough to permit (and reward) the deliberative overkill (ownership achieved at a snail's pace), inherent in this planning style, it can pay off. If you make the mistake, however, of using this type of strategic planning approach when you have a "Titanic" planning environment, it is nearly a certainty that all hands will go down with the ship—holding hands, smiling, and sharing the experience with each other, true; but nonetheless down with the ship!

3. Don't Throw Me in the Water Again, Coach. Some people have a highly developed *fear of failure,* and, when these people become executives, this fear, this need not to fail, drives the organization and patterns its strategic planning. The greatest fear of a person with a high fear of failure is, obviously, failing; and he or she does everything possible to avoid being placed in that situation. Translated into the long-range planning environment, this means not setting objectives (they may be the wrong ones), not taking risks (risk is a dirty word to people with a high fear of failure), and, when a choice is imperative, choosing strategic alternatives that minimize the risk of not meeting them. That means "safe" alternatives. (But executives with a high fear of failure often forget that there is no free lunch here either.)

In general, these executives tend to absent themselves from the strategic planning process—this done to leave themselves free of commitment, of measurable results, and therefore of any chance to fail. But how can they do this in a formal organizational setting? Let me count the ways! If the chief waits "too long" to choose organizational objectives, if he waits "too long" to size up the situation, if he waits "too long" to choose appropriately risky strategic alternatives, there's a fair chance that someone (or some group of second-level executives) will step in and do it for him—what we call in the trade a power vacuum. Another way! He can play "participative leader"—he can appoint numerous committees (with large memberships, please, to thoroughly diffuse responsibility for any screw-ups that may obtain) to "give him their advice" (make a decision) on the important facets of long-range planning. One more! He can be smart enough to have the right assistant to the president—an intelligent, ambitious, younger person who has the brains and drive to run the planning process and the common sense to treat the boss with the greatest deference, that is to let him stay on the public pedestal as president. One of my brightest MBAs in 20 years found himself in that very position three years ago. At the age of 27, he was actually managing a $30 million distributing company, including making hard strategic choices, while the president sat in the background, making occasional public and industry appearances. And they paid him plenty! My student let a good thing go to his head, however. One day an important industry figure called asking for the president. My MBA persuaded him *he* was the president "in fact"; the caller passed on this information to the real president, who in the only spark of managerial bravado observed in ten years promptly fired my boy. Moral: Even a cornered canary can defecate on you if he gets mad enough.

In a high-fear-of-failure organizational climate, the long-range planning that gets done, unless it is done extramurally, is of the fairly timid variety: low risk, short run (after all, if you look far enough into the future, you are bound to see something bad), hesitating, and often late. Executives with high fear of failure often hire a consultant to do the strategic long-range planning—this is to establish a convenient external locus for the guilt trip if things screw up. Those with an advanced case of the disease often hire two consultants—and then don't let either one know the other is doing it!

4. Nit-Picking Fault Finders and Fault-Finding Nit Pickers: Two Interesting Birds. When the Almighty was giving out brains and competence, he didn't specify that they should be rectangularly distributed, and, as a result, some people wind up as executives without the competence to do the job. Other people wind up with lots of competence but without a job (My MBA, for example). An incompetent executive who *knows* he's incompetent can manage very nicely, but an incompetent

THE NIT-PICKING FAULT-FINDER

executive who doesn't know it is a real 24-carat organizational menace. Here is an operating executive with a normal need to succeed, but without the means to succeed—a person for whom the great bright light of recognition never shines, the man or woman who doesn't get any strokes from other folks. What to do? Easy! Play organizational parasite, live off the mistakes of others. But how? Even easier! Find a bright, aggressive, organizationally minded, risk-taking executive and stand beside him or her. Sooner or later that person'll screw up. (All risk takers screw up sometimes; good executives don't often bat more than about .575 unless they are playing minor league executive ball and passing it off as major league stuff.) When he or she screws up, be the first to find it, be the first to report it, and make sure that everyone notices you did both. That's how the Nit-Picking Fault Finders and Fault-Finding Nit Pickers of this world survive, and that's how they make the great light shine on them. Sick, you say—right on!

But these clever psychological attackers do exist as an ornithological breed, and they do wind up in high organizational positions, and they do run companies, and good bird watchers must learn to recognize them by their habits and deal with them effectively. Attackers often quarrel with objectives that are set and with strategies that are chosen, finding *little* faults with them but never anything big. (They aren't bright enough to find anything big.) This is all part of laying the "I told you so" groundwork for making the great bright light shine later. Attackers don't take many risks, but they're always standing near someone who does, waiting! And they very cleverly keep themselves in a position where the choice of a particular strategy cannot be traced to them, a noncommittal nod, a carefully planned response that does not say "do it" but that doesn't say "don't do it" either. Neither do they tell their subordinates "how to do it" (how to implement a strategy). That reduces the chance to come back later and say "you did it wrong; you made a mistake." They are clever, though, and the subtle ones among them know how to pass this off by saying, "you are too competent for me to have to tell you what you should do." An insidious breed.

The long-range planning that results under this kind of a leader or in this kind of organizational climate is interesting—ineffective but interesting just the same. Whatever risk-taking behavior that does exist in the organization tends to get driven out. After all, who likes a public head chopping, especially when it's yours? If risks *are* taken, they are minor ones. And Roman messenger games are played to the hilt. No wonder. As soon as deviations from planned objectives are made visible, that is the signal for the attacker to get right to work. Deviations from past behavior are minimal too, because innovative behavior is a signal to the attacker that the chances for error are about to increase. And making errors visible is how the attacker exists. Of all the damage that this particular executive style does to the organization and its strategic long-range planning, none is more damaging than the subordination of the entrepreneurial (visionary) planning spark. That's what kills an organization quickest. Of course, this style is not without some merit, because it does give folks "down the line" a chance to practice their revolution planning skills.

For a while in the Air Force, I reported to one of these nit-picking types, a real wierdo named Talmage. He never made a suggestion that helped, but he criticized everything that my office did. One day in a conversation with him, I found out that he had once taught management (you could almost have guessed that). About a month later my office received a request from the University of Maryland College of Special Studies for an officer to teach management at Goose Bay, Labrador (the U.S. Air Force's own Isle of Elba). A sense of duty to the USAF propelled me to come in one Saturday and write an unsolicited recommendation for Major Talmage to a friend of mine at College Park, Maryland (a letter that was considerably better than my Ph.D. dissertation). Major Talmage left shortly thereafter for "Goose," as we called it, and I settled in to the happy business of running my purchasing office effectively.

5. *Do All Heroes Wear White Hats?* We've done a pretty good job in the last few pages of defining the bad guys. What do the good guys look like? Easy, they're the ones whose strategic planning systems work. (I am a measurer of outputs, you see.) No fair, you cry! Surely there must be an *a priori* normative model, a paradigm of the renaissance strategic planning top executive? Not even a short checklist to search and evaluate our future corporate president by? Cruel! Actually (ah, here it comes finally), a successful executive planner can come in many different forms, models, sizes, and attitudes, as long as he or she has enough need for achievement to set high objectives and take reasonable risks, enough personal humility to motivate his or her people to produce an honest size-up, enough self-confidence about his or her sense of the future to choose the right strategy today, and enough feel for the critical to know when to trade off ownership for speed and when not to. The rest is details! Oh yeah, forgot an important one—the successful planner has to have the honesty necessary to make his or her people believe in him or her, even when it ain't working right! (If you miss all these signs, look for a white hat. It never fails.)

ERROR VISIBILITY IN
LONG-RANGE PLANNING

Professors would rather be late than wrong. If you're wrong, 10,000 of your colleagues all over the world see that you were wrong. Other professors write rejoinders in the next ten issues of the journal to tell the world that you were wrong. Countless graduate students study all this generated literature to try to find out just how wrong you were, or why you went wrong, or how someone thought to be as smart as you could go so wrong, or why you are the only researcher who went wrong.

It's awful. As a result, being wrong in academe is a highly visible error. Being late isn't nearly as bad. Business is different; in business, it's always better to be vaguely right than precisely wrong.

Taking the Measure

All organizations measure things; it's part of the control process. Organizations spend tons of money perfecting their measuring systems. Steel mills measure the percentage of theoretical capacity reached, hospitals measure average occupancy, and airlines measure their load factor. Universities measure the number of publications by their faculty, and legislatures measure the number of classes that the faculties teach. The interesting thing about measuring systems, though, is that they raise things to *different* levels of visibility, sort of a selective perception measurement theory if you will. Measurement systems raise some things to very high levels of visibility: delinquent loans in banks, the number of industrial roofs that collapsed last year from snow loads, the number of unsuccessful new products introduced last year, the number of published items a faculty member has on his or her vita—all kinds of embarrassments get hoisted to the flag for all to see. And note that all these things are the results of actions that were *taken*. Most measuring systems are very good at measuring the results of things that we decided to do and then did.

But measuring systems are nearly always awful at measuring the results of opportunities *foregone*—of telling us how things we decided not to do would have turned out had we done them. For example, I don't know of very many banks that measure the money we could have made if we had not been so stingy in our lending decisions, that is, if we had loosened up our credit policy. And I don't know of many architects or engineering groups that measure the annual cost of overdesigning industrial roofs so that we will be certain they don't fall

119

down. And even the most advanced accountants are not very good at measuring profits that were lost from *not* introducing enough new products last year. And, thank goodness, no one really measures what else a professor could have done with all that time that he or she spent doing scholarly research.

Now, most executives are smart (that's a good bet most days). And, when the organization's measuring system gives these smart folks a choice between two errors (of about the same cost to the organization, let's say)—one that will be raised to a high level of visibility (excessive bad loans) and one that will remain at a nearly invisible level (the money that we are losing by not loosening up credit policy)—it's no wonder that smart executives quite naturally pick the less visible error, keeping credit policy tight.

In the small Southern town in which I was raised, the local banker preferred to make less visible errors, and credit policy was extremely tight, especially for farmers. A well-known local man (a nonbanker), Frank, spent most of his morning lounging in the lobby of the local bank. Each time a farmer was turned down for a loan, Frank would strike up a conversation with that farmer as he left the bank. Now Frank had a lot of money and didn't report to anybody; consequently, he wasn't afflicted by error visibility problems like the rest of the people who worked in the bank. Frank would lend money on most anything most anytime. But beware. Frank would foreclose on your farm if you were one day late on a $500 loan. When Frank died, he was worth more than the bank. Small wonder.

There is even some research indicating that executives have such a penchant for committing nearly invisible errors that they consistently do this even when the cost is *much* higher than is the cost of a highly visible error. After all, as a design engineer, how would you explain to your company that the warehouse roof that just collapsed in Memphis—the one you designed—was in fact part of an overall countrywide profit-maximizing design strategy for the company and that in fact the cost of repairing the Memphis roof was considerably less than all the money you saved by designing 50 warehouses that way for the last ten years? (Actually you shouldn't ever try to explain.) As a result, the controlling aphorism in design departments today is "when in doubt, make it stout"; a collapsed building is a very visible error, and it takes a real genius to explain that in fact it paid us to let it collapse!

Pro-Forming and Performing

Strategic long-range planning is the process of making risk-taking decisions in the face of an uncertain future, decisions that we hope will help us survive and even flourish down the road. Now everyone knows that "down the road" is hard to measure—hell, it's hard even to *see!* But *today* is easy to see, and therefore today is easy to measure; consequently, today gets measured a great deal more than "down the road." It turns out that executives in charge of designing measuring systems also know that there are only two errors they can make: (1) failing to measure the results of what we are doing today—*not performing* and (2) failing to measure the results "down the road" of things we are not doing today—not *pro-forming*. Accountants are much better at performing than pro-forming. What CPA could assuage the ignominy of failing to present this quarter's income statement by pointing out that he had spent the time instead in analysis, the results of which indicated that extrapolating our present strategy for five more years would likely result in our bankruptcy? Consequently, most accountants are conditioned to be very precise about today. Not very accurate about tomorrow—but always very precise about today!

Dancing to Different Tunes

Earlier in this chapter we pointed out that smart executives quickly learn "what gets counted here" and that they adjust their decision-making (risk-taking) behavior accordingly. In the context of the present discussion, this means simply that executives have their own penchant for committing nearly invisible errors, given half a chance.

At this point, the plot thickens. Many top executives really believe that it's their behavior alone—likes and dislikes, management style, do's and don't's, rewards and punishments they mete out—that controls the behavior of the organization below them. In fact, that's only partly true. Every organization has its own formal measuring system. This is quite different from the management *style* of its top executive. This system, as with all control systems, raises some behaviors to high levels of visibility and lets other behaviors stay nearly invisible. Executives in the organization know how to balance off these two factors: (1) the "atta boys" they get from the chief and (2) the formal report card they get from the measuring system and that gets in their file—at least the smart ones know how. If the chief wants consequential efforts put into "what we need to do today to get ready for an uncertain tomorrow," then it is his or her immutable responsibility to make sure that the measuring system illuminates (with maximum intensity) errors about tomorrow and simultaneously that it cloaks (in near invisibility) minor errors about today. Remember that personnel files and organizational folklore remain long after an appreciative chief moves on. What is measured gets written down, and behavior is conditioned by what is writ on stone tablets in the permanent file. All the more reason to make sure that the measuring system measures what it's supposed to. And, once more, it's the chief's responsibility to see that it does.

LET'S GET AWAY FROM IT ALL: RETREATS AND RETREATING

Once the planning process is about to get underway in an organization, it can benefit from some logistical tender loving forethought—no less than any other important activity that we want to be successful. In this regard, the strategic long-range planning retreat is becoming more and more common in organizations today. It makes good sense too. As industrial engineers were fond of pointing out years ago, all work is composed of two parts: (1) make ready and (2) do. "Make ready" involves getting your stuff together, getting to the workplace, deciding how and where to begin, and in general getting a "work" mindset in gear. "Do," on the other hand, is the process of accomplishing what has already been planned (and remember that it's done after the proper mindset had been established too).

Attempting to do meaningful strategic planning as an ordinary part of the normal working day is, in most environments, foolish. There are simply too many distracting elements. Or, to put it in industrial engineering parlance, you are forever repeating the "make ready" part of the work. Just as you are in the proper frame of mind with all your planning materials laid out, everything ready for some heavy skill work, here comes Mike with a question. OK, you answer the question, goodbye Mike, you get back in a planning mindset—and here comes an emergency phone call. It'll happen that way every time. You are always repeating the "make ready" part of long-range planning at the expense of the "do" part. Result: Not a hell of a lot gets done.

So consider the long-range planning retreat, an attempt to get the seminal thinkers in the organization away from their normal working environment, away from the interruptions, and into an environment in which "make ready" for strategic planning is done only once. A few years ago I was invited to a West African country to spend a couple of weeks with cabinet officials in such a planning retreat. The site selected was several hundred miles from the capital city, a distance thought sufficient to discourage visits home (or home visits there). The retreat village had no telephone either; some enterprising crew had come in and in one night ripped off 11 miles of copper telephone wire. The ministers arrived in their cars. I came in by helicopter, and we went to work, uninterrupted. At dinner the first evening, one of the ministers introduced me to his niece, a very attractive young lady of about 19. The next evening, three more ministers introduced me to their nieces. By the end of the first week, there were 22 nieces present at the retreat. For the first two nights, I was terribly impressed with the family devotion implied in a trip of that arduousness by women so young. By the third day, I had it figured out!

One problem with *retreats* is that they often turn out to be *retreating*, that is, withdrawing from the problems of an organization to a more idyllic environment and promptly forgetting why we are there (nieces and all that). In fact, however, long-range planning retreats involve some of the hardest work that people can do in an organization. To consider one a paid vacation and to treat it lightly is a serious error, fun today but trouble tomorrow! A successful long-range planning retreat involves a great deal of planning itself as well as consequential commitment to the process and outcome by each participant, before, during, and after the actual retreat.

Sightseeing Only After 2 P.M.

Plan the retreat itself *before* you leave home. It's poor form and grossly inefficient to show up at the long-range planning retreat and begin to plan what you'll do there. My own experience assigns high marks to an outline and timetable published before anyone leaves home, indicating just what we intend to do. This serves several important purposes. First, it eliminates useless arguments about "form"—what we'll do first, and second, and third, and so on. Second, it sets targets of accomplishment and thus improves our chances of reaching these targets. Third, it cuts down the bullshit about extraneous topics. I've observed that whenever you get a high-powered bunch of people together in a nice environment, away from all the mundane issues of running an organization, and ask them to consider futures, that setup presents an almost unavoidable temptation to bullshit. Bullshitting with intelligent people about where we ought to be ten years from today is a lot of fun, awfully stimulating, and sometimes unavoidable. Granted, we are at the retreat to do creative dreaming. But the difference between creative dreaming and bullshit is focus. So publish an outline, focus sharp, and knock off the bullshit.

Long-range planning retreats that continue all day are generally a bust. It's hard enough working at your desk all day back at the office—what makes people think that the creative spark can be maintained for eight continuous hours when the topic is as important and mentally demanding as "what we ought to be when we grow up"? My own experience is that an early start (before 8 A.M.), a hell-bent effort till about 1 P.M., then a recreation break till 5 P.M., then a plenary meeting for an hour on what we'll do tomorrow, then cocktails, dinner, and an evening off makes for a good pattern. You might hit on another good schedule. But what must be avoided at all costs here is an overzealous, budgetary-minded chief executive (or an underbrained budgetary-minded personnel clerk or budget officer) worrying about the cost of all this talent and trying to minimize said cost by scheduling ten hours of work with a three-hour evening session. Just won't work in most cases. You know, thinking long versus thinking short!

Before You Leave Home
Be Sure to . . .

I've never had any success running a long-range planning retreat without requiring some advance work of the participants. Last year I was asked to conduct a long-range planning retreat for a $10-million manufacturer of ladies' dresses. The company had budgeted three days for the retreat at a very posh resort hotel on the East Coast. A month before the retreat was scheduled to begin, I sent to each of the nine corporate officers who were to attend a short questionnaire designed to gather information about where each of them was coming from and where each one of them thought the company was going. I asked each of them to send the completed questionnaire back to *me* unsigned at least a week before the retreat so I could tabulate results for all to see. Here is an edited version of the questionnaire.

1. First your best guess as to where the company will be:

	in 5 years	in 10 years
Sales volume, in units	_____	_____
Sales volume, in dollars	_____	_____
Number of production locations	_____	_____
Number of employees	_____	_____
Return on sales	_____	_____
Return on assets	_____	_____
Return on equity	_____	_____

2. Next your thoughts for product line changes in the next few years; put a check under the appropriate column in each instance.

	Agree	Disagree	Not sure
a. The lines will stay about the same	_____	_____	_____
b. Need to broaden the lines			
(1) older styles	_____	_____	_____
(2) younger styles	_____	_____	_____
(3) coordinates	_____	_____	_____
(4) add related items	_____	_____	_____
(a) made by us	_____	_____	_____
(b) made by others	_____	_____	_____
c. Add offshore production	_____	_____	_____
d. Develop private-label business	_____	_____	_____

3. Another way to look at our product line is to divide it into broad categories; please do that, and for each category give us your expectations for the future (units, please, as inflation would make dollar forecasts tricky).

Category Description	I expect the percentage increase or decrease for this category to be	
	In 5 years	In 10 years
Category A _____	_____	_____
Category B _____	_____	_____
Category C _____	_____	_____
Category D _____	_____	_____
Category E _____	_____	_____
Category F _____	_____	_____

4. Now please give us an idea of your current time allocations and your expected time allocations for the future.

	Now	In 5 years
a. Weekly hours you work	_____	_____
b. Number of out-of-town trips per month	_____	_____
c. Mix of your total time	_____	_____
(1) corporate	_____%	_____%
(2) civic	_____%	_____%
(3) family/leisure/recreation	_____%	_____%
	100%	100%

5. Looking ahead, write your opinion of the major differences that will have to take place in our business if we are to be successful five or ten years from now.

6. Over the next five to ten years, what new skills, if any, will the company need to be successful?

7. What limitations (human, financial, external, etc.) do you see standing in the way of us reaching our goals in the next five years?

Why did we do this questionnaire and what do we have when we're done? First, we have a composite sense of felt corporate objectives by the company's senior executives. From this we can quickly see whether we have diversity or congruence in objectives and whether this diversity or congruence is toward or away from objectives toward which we *should* be working. Next we have a good quick sense of how our people feel about the markets that we serve, both in a general sense and later in a more specific sense. Third, we have information on the kinds of personal commitments that our people see themselves making to the organization over the planning horizon. Finally, we have some individual positions on changes likely to obtain in our business and industry, weaknesses within the firm that need correcting, and internal and external constraints we need to focus on. Having this information already tabulated when we begin eliminates a whole lot of non-directional talk, indicates what kind of consensus there is among the top executives as to the way things *are* and *ought to be,* and offers a quickly focused view of what people think the major problems here really are. For a few hours' investment of time by each executive, we have introduced some form and direction to our long-range planning retreat. (And you know what that cuts down.)

The anonymity deserves a special note. Why, you ask, are these sent in to a third party anonymously? In fact, it isn't strictly necessary. I find, however, that you get a lot less political positioning, a lot more honesty, a more candid illumination of constraints, and a much better (noncompany-line) view of the marketplace when you do it this way. In fact, if the retreat environment is open, if the discussions are without acrimony, if seemingly nutty ideas are listened to with respect, and if the chief has his behavioral hat on, all or most of the individual written and anonymous inputs will become *ad hominem* during the discussions anyhow. Anonymity just happens to be an effective, nondefensive way to start. Oh, yes, the president is required to submit his questionnaire too; otherwise it's not a fair game!

From Theory to Practice

My wife Charlotte and I were touring the Soviet Union a few years ago and decided to go home a couple of days early. I walked from our hotel on Gorki Avenue down to the Intourist

Office on Red Square and called for my Intourist agent, a young dedicated party worker named Talotin. After about half an hour he came down and I told him we wanted to go to Vienna tomorrow, instead of Saturday. He sat there completely deflated by my request—really in a depressed state. My God, I thought, I didn't ask him for an audience with Breshnev, just a change in an airline flight. But Talotin sat there not answering. Finally, the silence killing me, I said in a tone only mildly critical of the Soviet bureaucracy, Mr. Talotin, *is* it possible in this country to change an airline reservation? He looked back at me and in the nearest manner to real humor I had heard in Russia said, "Professor Levin, in theory it's possible."

Going from theory to successful practice in a long-range planning retreat requires some mechanical props (schedules, quiet, location, preretreat questionnaires, etc.) and some behavioral props (openness, honesty, group cohesiveness, etc.). If the behavioral props don't exist *before* the retreat, they aren't likely to emerge *during* it. However, there *are* some mechanical issues about scheduling that may be of some help. This is a schedule that was followed fairly successfully during the long-range planning retreat for the dress manufacturing outfit—no paradigm of efficiency or all-purpose model, just a commonsense approach. The president's name is Jimmy, the company shall remain nameless.

Tentative Outline for June Retreat

1. Wednesday: What is long-range planning? (30 minutes to 1 hour)

    a. Discussion of advance reading on long-range planning

    b. The meaning of long-range planning to the company and its executives

    c. Corporate versus personal long-range planning (what's the relationship?)

    d. What we'll try to accomplish in these three days

2. Wednesday: The company planning environment over the next ten years—the way our world will be (3 to 3½ hours)

    a. Jimmy's views of the future with some numbers to think about

        (1) past corporate strategy and how well it's done

        (2) some growth figures for sales, past and future

        (3) sales by major product line, trends

        (4) equity assumptions (for nonfamily members)

        (5) how we'll finance growth

        (6) number of top-level organizational positions that will be opened through growth (various growth rates/plans)

        (7) necessary qualifications (education/drive/attitude/experience) for those top-level positions

        (8) major constraints (internal and external) to implementing the various strategies open to the company

        (9) Jimmy's personal feelings and plans

    b. A composite of the other participants' views (tabulated from anonymous replies to our preretreat questionnaire)

        (1) where they see the company going over the next ten years

        (2) where they see themselves going over the same period

        (3) what kinds of gaps this discloses between (1) and (2)

        (4) implied gaps in their experience/education/attitudes

        (5) the fit between them and the company for ten years

        (6) the major constraints to goal achievement they see over the next ten years

        (7) the half dozen or so specific problems they see the company having in the next one to five years

3. Thursday: Specific force-field analysis of the major strategic alternatives open to the company (each alternative tested against internal and external constraints) (1 to 1½ hours)

> a. Examination of both the personal and the corporate costs and benefits of strategies illuminated on Wednesday
> b. Which of the strategies appear to be foreclosed by the individual "preference sets" (executives' wishes) disclosed on Wednesday?
> c. Which of the strategies appear to be foreclosed by the corporate "marketing/finance" problems disclosed on Wednesday?

4. Thursday: Workable strategic alternatives that seem to be left when we take into account our executives' wishes, possible growth alternatives, markets, and finance (1 to 1½ hours)

> a. Static volume with the same executive crew
> b. Growth plans with the same executive crew
> c. Growth plans with an augmented executive crew
> d. Growth plans with a predominately new executive crew
> e. Selling out

5. Friday: Where do we go from here? (2 hours)

> a. Do we seem to have chosen 4a or 4e above; if so, what next?
> b. Which constraints need to be moved for 4b, 4c, or 4d to take place?
> > (1) inside ones
> > (2) outside ones
> c. Specific market/product line plans we should consider

    d. Organizational and personnel changes that seem to be
      necessary
    e. Timetables that seem reasonable for us
    f. Follow-up—when should we look at this again?
    g. Do we have commitment?

Nuff said on schedule and props—make ready. The rest is doing.

BEHAVIORAL ODDS AND ENDS:
LAME DUCKS AND ALL
THAT STUFF

Lame duck presidents have been curious objects for historians' research for years and years. Lame duck chief executives of any organization have real problems. In this instance let's talk briefly about two—*timing* and *protection.* Executives with limited tenure (those about to be promoted, those about to be demoted, those about to retire, those about to leave) have a difficult time with strategic long-range planning. First, if your tenure with the organization is involuntarily short, you have little motivation to think big thoughts for this bunch of ingrates. Second, if your tenure with this organization is voluntarily short, your remaining days are no time to commence anything as consequential as a strategic long-range planning effort. You simply can't get the commitment you need to pull it off, you certainly don't have the time, and a hurried effort with no commitment is a hell of a poor way to exit. Third, initiating a long-range planning effort in the face of an incoming chief executive wastes your time, mortgages his or her effectiveness, and confuses the troops. It's kind of like trying to teach a pig to play the violin. It's very difficult to do and it annoys the hell out of the pig!

Now to the *protection.* For long-range planning to work, it has to have the commitment of the executives in an organization; ownership is the key. And of course, by definition, long-range planning is risk-taking behavior, and, for executives to take risks, they must have some assurance of protection from their boss before they take these risks—it's only fair! With the departure of the chief executive imminent, to whom do they look for protection from the risks that they are being asked to take? If the answer to that question is moot, it's obvious that they will not take the "right kind" of risks or make the honest kinds of sizing up assessments necessary to make long-range planning a success. So why do it?

A Man For Each Season Is Better

The concept of a renaissance strategic planner at the helm for all seasons is basically a crock. Organizations that forget to link executive assignments with the company's strategic needs at the time are making a tragic mistake. Consider the cowboy entrepreneur who drove the company from $1 million to $10 million in just five years, (and the suppliers and the banks all the way). Is that really the person best suited to coach the organization as it plans for the mature stage of its product cycle? Do 185 pound quarterbacks make good defensive guards? Not so! The entrepreneur wins his spurs making something out of nothing, taking risks, pushing the team in the tough years, running hard and lean. Milking a "cash cow" successfully is quite another ball game (and consequently needs a new coach to win).

Look at how a couple of well run organizations successfully played the "man for each season game." First Heublein. This corporation divided up its United Vintners wine business into two parts a few years back, a premium wine division and a standard wine division. To head the premium wine division, they chose their knowledgeable wine marketing vice president, Robert Furek, a "pro" who understood how to plan for quality over volume. To coach the standard wine division the company chose Harold Spielberg, a former personal products manager for Gillette, a man who understood well how to plan for aggressive pricing and volume. A neat match of talents and needs.

133

Now a tale where the outcome isn't as rosy. Texas Instruments failed to follow through on its early lead in integrated circuits in part because it missed the call on the management style necessary to make the organization go. TI began its foray into integrated circuits twenty years ago with the scientific developer of the product, Jack Kilby, subordinate to the product line manager, a seasoned administrative type. A couple of years later, the administrative type was moved out in favor of the more scientific Kilby who stressed research at the expense of financial controls. This led to Kilby's being eased out a few years later, back to the research lab. As tighter financial controls were implemented TI began to realize, albeit too late, that Kilby's scientific orientation was exactly what was needed; the management types just couldn't muster the *technical* muscle to get the line going. In 1967 the head of TI's semiconductor operations exchanged management again; this time they brought in a technically oriented bunch. A game of musical chairs yes, but not the right match of strategic mindset and organizational needs at any one time. TI admits this was a costly game.

When It Hits the Fan

No one ever said that long-range planning had a high chance of success, but then if you could hit just .360 you could have won the American League batting championship in 1979! Screw-ups are inevitable, and they will happen no matter how elegant the long-range planning process or how much time you put into implementation either. So screw up it will. When that happens, the executive has several places to point at for the culprit: (1) the environment, a willing and cooperative goat any year; (2) other people, careful here—if they're inside, they can save up "gotchas payable" against you, and, besides, they're all you have to work with anyhow; (3) people outside, attractive but dangerous, as folks will likely ask why these outsiders didn't similarly affect the competition; (4) yourself, a noble action reserved for stalwart chief executives; or (5) the long-range planning process, the most dangerous ploy of all. Don't kill the goose just because someone stepped on one of her eggs! You will need the process for a long time to come. If you demean it, all the people who participated in that process will be more leary next time around. Go on and be a hero—it don't hurt long!

If it screws up, take a cue from a major electronics company and from the movie *The Exorcist*. Our electronics giant lost half a billion dollars in one year monkeying around in the computer business. When the chips were down and it was clear they had been stomped, they handled the guilt like gentlemen. They found a low-level, unsuspecting, nearly uninvolved financial executive; then they took a big broom and swept all the guilt in one pile. Then they packaged it very neatly and tied it with a ribbon, then they fastened it around the neck of that poor man, and then they fired him. (Actually the way it came out was "early retirement.") Foul, you cry, American capitalism on the rampage again! Probably so, but look how clean it left the rest of the troops to try again. Guilt kills an organization's will to plan again. One good exorcism is worth five years of penance any day!

SIX

Long-Range
Planning
In Different
Environments

A plan for all seasons . . .
alligators and quick sand too.

A plan . . . is a plan . . . is a plan.

(What Gertrude Stein would have said
if she'd gone to business school)

And planning is planning in all seasons and weathers, for little organizations, big ones, and individuals; for make-money concerns and nonprofit groups; for new or old, illicit or legitimate, mainstream or underground, local, national, or international ventures—for one and all, the strategic long-range planning process is the same. And it works. A strategy is just a plan for getting from here to there, no matter who you are. So if you want to go, you take a look at yourself, you glance around the environment, you fix your eye on the objective, and you sit down in a quiet corner and calculate the best way to get there. Pretty simple concept. (Aren't they all, though? Of course, the implementation may drive you bananas, but that's beyond the scope of this book. Which is why it's called a primer.)

There *are* special cases, however, with pitfalls for the unwary. Although the planning process is the same, the hazards are different—you know, alligators on the fourth hole in Florida, quicksand beside the seventeenth tee in Louisiana. So let me just give you a few quick insights into six situations that I've encountered: planning with scientists, for government and nonprofit concerns, for contingencies, for new ventures, in inflationary conditions, and for one's own career. This chapter is an invitation to stand on my shoulders while we walk the course, studying quicksand and alligators. Alley-oop!

LONG-RANGE PLANNING IN
SCIENTIFIC ENVIRONMENTS

But We're Different

Scientists (and other assorted heavy technical types) have aspirations just like the rest of us. They want to develop themselves beyond narrow technical spheres; they desire recognition in their scientific specialty; many of them even

138

want to *manage* scientific endeavors instead of just being a cog. That's where the problem begins.

Most scientists who work in basic fields such as biology, chemistry, and physics or in applied areas such as environmental analysis, energy, and medicine have generally been trained to reason *inductively*, to plod along carefully from one proven fact to another proven fact until in due course they either do or don't state that some conclusion is true. In science it is the rule to be careful, deliberative, and slow—and a very rewarding rule too; remember that, when a scientist is wrong and publishes an incorrect conclusion, all hell breaks loose. Taking early unsubstantiated public positions on the issue is poor scientific form. A scientist is trained and rewarded for making no decision, that is, for staying neutral about his or her findings, until those findings are fully supported with statistically significant research.

Hunch—or seat-of-the-pants—decision making, however valuable in higher-order endeavors such as fishing, bird hunting, or playing the market, has no place in science. About the worst thing that a scientist can do is to overgeneralize about the usefulness or validity of what he or she has already found. And, of course, one of the most legitimate answers in science is "we don't know yet; we're still researching it." That answer is acceptable, honest, and respectable; and, if you forget time frames, it has operational significance. It simply means that things are moving along the right path of scientific inquiry but that we're not ready to say any more than that now. Honorable circumspection.

Different From Whom?

Managers are different from scientists, different in training and behavior. From their first day in an MBA program or on their first job, managers either are taught or quickly find that they are forever making decisions *without* complete research, that most of their really consequential decisions are based on insufficient data, and that, if they wait until the issue at question has been fully researched, the financial opportunity generally disappears along with the need for the decision.

Managers—at least the successful ones—tend to get used to this time-uncertainty crucible. Their training is basically *deductive*: they draw conclusions, often correct ones, from those wonderful absolute certainties known to be true, such as (1) people work harder when they're treated fairly; (2) you must take in enough money to cover all expenses; (3) buy low, sell high; and (4) the competition is never quite as dumb as you think. Deductive thinking is *great* as long as the "principles" on which you base your decisions turn out to be right most of the time. Notice that it is not necessary that these "principles" be right all of the time, only *most of the time*.

The manager is hard pressed to get away with answering, "we don't know yet; we're still researching it"—at least any manager who makes really consequential decisions. Regardless of the uncertainty attached to next year's forecast of GNP, sales, and interest rates, somebody must make production and inventory decisions *now* and put money on the line today. "I don't know" is not only unacceptable in most for-profit organizational settings; it has downright negative connotations for job security.

A Million Here, a Million There,
or Bond Trading in the Big City

I have a friend named George who buys and sells bonds for a financial house. He deals in millions and millions of dollars every day. Some days he misses it. George screws up—you call it what you want, but maybe George stays in an issue ten minutes too long, or maybe he just misreads the "trail signs." Anyhow, George gets on the 6:07 to Stamford, having lost his company a quarter of a million dollars today. He goes home, kisses his wife and two kids, has a drink and dinner, watches a little T.V., reads a bit, then goes to bed. The next morning, George shows up at work with the same intuitive equipment he had the day before. George has no greater research potential than he had yesterday, and certainly no additional scientific facts about the behavior of bonds, and is still expected to do his deals. So George gets on the phone and does it again. Today maybe he wins or maybe he loses another quarter million or so — in the long run he wins or he's out!

Now kindly observe my friend Mack, a professor of financial theory at a Southern university. Mack teaches a couple of graduate courses in advanced financial theory, does extensive research on "Prediction Characteristics of Bond Price Fluctuations," and has his money socked away in the local savings and loan. Mack would last one hour trading bonds. If the market didn't get him, the Maalox would! George would last about two weeks teaching "Bond Trading." The graduate students with their horrible penchant for focusing on inputs would be unable to understand how George does it successfully *without* theoretical models, would tire of hearing *how* he made $8 million last year for his company, and would quietly leave the class. Then the Maalox would get George, too!

Macks Get Promoted Too

Mack gets strokes just like George gets strokes; Mack gets his from "making a contribution to human knowledge" (as it says in the tenure handbook). George, on the other hand, isn't expected to push knowledge ahead rapidly, just to make money by trading bonds for the company. You know—buy low, sell high. The Macks of this world sometimes become managers. And, although *management* and *managing* are, respectively, (1) beyond their ability to prove and (2) outside their sphere of competence, managers they do become. And, in spite of the fact that their largely inductive training does little to prepare them for the largely deductive world they face, face it they do.

141

In my experience, scientists tend to be mechanical managers, therefore mechanical long-range planners. Upon checking out five or six articles and books on the subject, reading them carefully, and taking copious notes, they have great difficulty understanding how books and articles on long-range planning written by three different "Georges" can differ in methodology: "Isn't there an accepted theory of planning?" "My God, you mean you management types have been practicing it for 2,000 years, writing about it for 50 years, and doing research on it for 10 years, and there is *still* no agreement on what it is?" More Maalox!

Scientists get captivated by *diagrams* in long-range planning. They love anything that adds scientific oomph to a managerial world they see as bereft of science. In the 1960s, scientists in Washington went ape over the systems theory approach to management (after all, it *was* developed by a biologist). They take Drucker lightly. His stuff has very few footnotes, and, besides, he uses too many anecdotes—like my friend George! Their tastes in long-range planning literature run toward scholarly pieces with new terminology, new taxonomies of planning phenomena, and statistically significant tests of hypotheses at the .01 confidence level—oh, yes, and lots of diagrams!

When it comes to handling speed and risk in long-range planning, scientific organizations are afflicted with turtle blood. Most scientists operate in a world not visibly attuned to timetables, fiscal years, or urgency. Remember, scientists are trained to take whatever precautions are required to ensure that they are *not* wrong; successful managers on the other hand are often wrong, but they are *never* in doubt. Scientific organizations must face risk just like any other, and in many instances the risk will not diminish as a result of extended "scientific" examination of the problem. Helping the scientific organization to make timely risk-taking planning decisions (or helping them to recognize the risks inherent in decisions that they are avoiding today) is a formidable task indeed.

Here are a few assorted suggestions for dealing with the long-range planning process in organizations of scientists:

1. Keep planning meetings short. Scientists tend to treat them as conferences anyhow, and unherded discourse is their stock in trade. They can go on for hours, and hours, and hours, and hours.

2. Give everybody something to read on planning beforehand. Copy and distribute the most scientific-sounding piece you can find on the subject just to get them started talking.

3. Get a speaker for the first long-range planning meeting, preferably one of those management scientists with a long vita. It doesn't matter much what he or she says.

4. Set out complete time schedules, target dates, and intermediate points from the beginning. If you leave the planning open–ended, that's the way it will turn out. Make sure schedules and target dates get into print sooner or later.

5. Don't try for broad general agreement on too wide a topic. That's not the way scientists operate anyhow. Get agreement on small bits and pieces each time. Put these together yourself into larger pieces before the next meeting. That's the way scientists do research—that's the way they think.

6. Spread the planning risk as much as you can. Don't let it be vested with only one member of the planning process. Let the process, not an individual, make the long-range planning decisions. They call that a "jointly authored publication" in the trade.

7. Watch and control the attackers. With their copious notes, they will kill the folks willing to take risks. Don't let them play "on September 19th last year you said." That's a bad game.

8. Write complete minutes and distribute them soon after each planning meeting, inviting all who attended to add,

delete, or correct. This is part of a scientist's ownership process.

9. Make the final long-range plan fairly lengthy, as so much input should generate a lot of output. Because the long-range planning process will have gone on to fruition before the plan is written anyhow, the effect of the length on performance is inconsequential.

10. Have something in the written plan from everyone on the planning committee or in the planning process. It's called "the old boy citation game."

11. Scientists love form; behavioral gimmicks seem to freak them out. Try mirror groups, matrix organization formats, task teams, and simulation. It will help get ownership of the process. Even if they don't like *what* they're doing, they'll like *how*.

12. Remember, each long-range planning meeting is in reality a scientific conference. Everyone there must listen attentively to everyone's scientific paper. That's a rule!

LONG-RANGE PLANNING IN GOVERNMENTAL AND NOT-FOR-PROFIT ORGANIZATIONS

Only the Name's Changed

When I was in graduate school, I had a dance orchestra. One night after we had played at the Hickory Country Club, we were involved in a particularly grinding auto accident and wound up (actually we woke up) at a small county hospital near Newton, North Carolina operated by three very likeable physicians. Being a student, I used my three weeks there to observe how these gentlemen operated their hospital. I noticed very definite patterns in patient-load characteristics apparently correlated to which day of the week it was. Children seemed to appear most on Wednesdays, older people on Tuesdays, with very few new patients at all on Thursdays. I was most impressed with the efficiency at this hospital, so I asked one of the

144

nurses about this interesting arrival pattern of patients. Oh, she said, Tuesday is "hickey day." "Hickey day?" I asked. "Oh, you know," she said, "those little warts and skin tags that grow on older folks. Well, the doctors like to take them all off on Tuesday, so we call Tuesday hickey day." "Well, what about Wednesday," I said, "why so many kids?" "That's tonsil day," she said. "If we do them all on Wednesday, they can be out before the weekend." Impressed, I continued. "Why is Thursday so slack?" "Oh," she replied, "all three doctors always play golf on Thursday." Moral: If HEW could devise such a simple yet effective system, we all might have a chance.

The political process and the planning process do not cohabitate without plenty of accomodation of the latter to the former. The accommodation of planning to the realities of government begins with careful choice of time horizons. In Chapter 4, we noted these five general characteristics of planning horizons: (1) they are not fixed, (2) longer horizons are not always better, (3) planning horizons change over time in response to the rate of change in the environment, (4) different decisions require different horizons, and (5) horizons tend to become shorter as we go further down in the organization. Each of these *general* characteristics applies equally well to the not-for-profit organization, but, in addition, the unique nature of not-for-profit organizations generates some *specific* time horizon problems.

A few years ago, I addressed a group of 30 cabinet- and subcabinet-level members of a state government on the subject of long-range planning. As is my custom, I began with a few general questions to the group to loosen them up and give me some sense of their thinking on planning. First question: "How many of you have a five-year plan in some written form?" Not a hand went up. "OK" I said, "how many of you have a one-year plan in written form?" Still not a hand went up. Triumphant, and now ready to make the case for long-range planning, I asked them why they didn't have written plans. "Oh," they said, "we do, we do, but you didn't ask how many have a two-year plan." "OK, why two years?" I asked, clearly rattled at being one-upped at this point. "Because that's the period that the

145

state legislature appropriates money for, and we don't think it makes sense to plan beyond your money supply." It was not one of my better talks. I made it through an hour or so of general nonsense on long-range planning with half of my mind driving my voice and the other half wondering just who in heaven's name in that group worried and planned for issues with time horizons longer than two years—a category probably pretty crowded.

Most countries, states, cities, and other governmental units are headed by a person appointed or elected for a specific limited term of office. Unfortunately, this fact tends to focus long-range planning time horizons on the tenure of the appointed or elected officials. You can see the peril to long-term organizational health. It is pure foolishness to believe that one four-year term, for example, is any kind of universally appropriate planning horizon. True, this four-year term may turn out to be the focus for many plans and programs, and it usually carries with it a significant change of top administrators; nevertheless, the organization's mission, its clients, its special interest groups, and its constituents demand planning horizons both shorter *and* longer than a four-year fixed parameter. Planning for long-run organizational needs and changes, for example, in manpower, structure, and training to name but a few, goes *beyond* four years, if we want to maintain organizational viability and creativity. It is equally foolish to force a four-year planning horizon on lower-level activities of a government organization merely because that's the term of office of the elected official higher up, and his political appointees.

A simple fact of life: Changes in the environment do not necessarily coincide with changes in the administration of a governmental organization. Organizations plan in response to their environment, and they choose planning horizons in terms of how rapidly they see their environment changing. Election laws, on the other hand, stick with fixed horizons; it is therefore purely coincidental to see a change in administration, with its attendant refocusing of planning and planning goals, occur simultaneously with the consequential environmental changes that require extended planning horizons. Incoming administrators plan for *their* tenure (and a bit beyond if they are real statespersons), and the environment moves onward despite election outcomes. Precisely for that reason, organizations must generate time frames for planning that are more realistic for their environment.

Musical Chairs—Plan, Plan,
Who's Got the Plan?

We've already related long-range planning time horizons in government to the term of office of elected officials. Let's expand on that a bit to the case of "remaining tenure." Ever since I lived in Turkey thirteen years ago, I have followed Turkish politics with fond interest. During my time there, I helped the Turks initiate a management training program for their civil service; naturally, this involved politics. If you look at Turkish national elections over the last ten years, you find two prime ministers playing musical chairs, Bulent Ecevit and Suleyman Demirel. Both gentlemen are capable, and both have the long-run needs of their country at heart, but neither has made even a small dent in the tragic condition of their country over the last ten years. Maybe the economic and social problems aren't solvable, you say. Rubbish! The solutions are well known to both Ecevit and Demirel. Well, then maybe the resources are just not available for their solution. Not so! The IMF, OECD, UN, the United States, and a host of other national and international bodies have pledged resources ample to implement a solution to Turkey's problems. Well, what's the problem then? It's a clear case of "remaining tenure" disease. With a flexible elections law (the "outs" can challenge the "ins" whenever they feel that things aren't going well), the newly elected prime minister focuses on two actions, both with extremely short-run planning horizons: (1) getting his friends into cabinet and subcabinet posts as quickly as possible and

147

(2) avoiding actions that will antagonize any subset of the electorate such as collecting taxes from the wealthy, reorganizing government, enforcing trade and monetary laws, modernizing education, and stimulating long-run investment. The permanent lower-level civil service, meanwhile, sits by and observes this game of musical chairs and, fearful of its own "guaranteed" tenure, does nothing but run through the day-to-day drill of "keeping the doors open." Result: Most if not all of the long-run issues begging for enlightened planning are finessed in the name of staying elected, because, if we antagonize any constituent group, out we go. The result is continuous and built-in instability at the top level of government, no meaningful attention to longer-run planning horizons, a massive C.Y.A. (old Southern expression . . .) effort by the civil service, and a country verging on disaster.

The "remaining tenure" notion is not the sole province of underdeveloped countries. All elected politicians tend to *increase* their long-range planning focus up until the day that they are elected, at which time (1) planning time horizons get reduced immediately (this is nothing more than realizing that election promises are just that and nothing more), and (2) focus begins to shift to those plans and programs that can bear some political fruit during the incumbent's tenure. There is nothing fundamentally bad about the system *as long as* somebody, some group, or some institution continuously focuses on the longer-run, permanent, ongoing needs of the constituents and of the organization itself. In our national system, the Congress, with its staggered approach to minimizing the effects of "remaining tenure syndrome," provides some of the stewardship of longer-run planning horizons ("beyond this administration"), and the permanent civil service provides much of the "beyond this administration" recharging of the organization itself. As long as *some* workable provision is made for handling and responding to "beyond tenure" long-range planning horizons, the consequential issues facing governments will continue to be addressed and sometimes even solved.

All governments implement *programs*. The food stamp program, the save the cities program, the clean up Sheboygan program, the wheat subsidy program, the stamp out venereal disease program—all these are focused responses to perceived societal needs. That's the stuff that administrations are made of. But is it the stuff that *governments* are made of? Conventional wisdom says no. Programs are what a government organization does to implement strategies approved or initiated by elected officials. But all these programs depend for their success upon a governmental organization able to administer them effectively. It's kind of like the radio business. If you've got great programming, but your sales and technical staff are the pits, you get stomped by your creditors. It's also a certainty that if you have a splendid sales staff and technical crew, and your programming is the pits, you get stomped by your listeners. Elected representatives focus mainly on governmental programming. That's not bad unless the permanent members of the organization (the civil service so to speak) begin to think that all these programs laid end to end represent the aggregate long-range plan for the organization. That's a myth. These programs are the long-range plan for serving constituents. But in no sense do they represent the long-range plan for the organization itself. The ability of governmental organizations to implement, that is, their ability to put ideas into practice, is almost always divorced from the programs (ideas) themselves. Programs allocate money, never ability. Implementive ability is instead vested in the permanent cadre of nonelected officials and is a direct function of how well they do their long-range planning. Roughly, the politician proposes, the civil service disposes.

Planning for implementive ability doesn't focus on programs, but on organizational needs. An effective long-range plan for a governmental agency need not contain a single reference to a specific program. Instead, the relevant focus of governmental agency planning is on things such as (1) *Effectiveness of service:* How well is your agency satisfying client demand given the existing constraints? This question asks in fact whether you have a market research system in operation and whether you know how to use some kind of benefit–cost analysis to optimize resource use. (2) *Productivity:* How effective is your organization in delivering services? Are the delivery procedures cost–effective? Do you measure and compare productivity? (3) *Organizational stability and viability:* Is your agency organized in the most effective manner given the programs that you implement? Is your organizational structure designed to carry out functions effectively? What is the extent of training carried on by your agency? Is the delegation of authority in your agency sufficient to get maximum decision-making power from the organization? (4) *Organizational climate:* Do the people in your organization work effectively as a team? Are the communication procedures adequate? Do you monitor the organizational climate? How do you go about assessing it and identifying problems with it? (5) *External relationships:* How well does your agency relate to (a) the people who originate the programs you implement, (b) the clients whom these programs serve, and (c) the special interest groups in the environment? (6) *Competition:* What regulatory, political, and social changes can you see in the environment that will increase the competition that your agency now faces in its "public marketplace"?

The Exogenous Revolving Door

Government types are fond of complaining about the changes in administration that characterise our imperfect democracy every four years or so. A favorite pastime is for several sub-cabinet level officers to get together and rationalize away their failure to plan on the grounds that "the changes in leadership are like a revolving door, and all we can do is watch and wait. After all, who could reasonably be expected to plan in the face of such persistent uncertainty?" This adult form of the self pity game "Gee Ain't It Awful" is just that, self pity.

The revolving door nature of elected leadership is *not* an exogenous variable to the planning process; it is an integral part of the plan and must be treated as such for any progress to be made. Making it exogenous only serves to rationalize our failure to deal with it, and consequently any failures which obtain because we chose to disregard it.

If changes in leadership at the top scramble your administrative life, then the practical planner concentrates on workable plans to (1) size up the incoming leadership faster (2) present the incoming leadership with the real administrative and political alternatives open to his or her decisions (3) build the flexibility into the organization necessary to tolerate and thrive on change, and (4) weed out those folks who would rather play "Gee, Ain't It Awful".

There is a whole list of organizational issues which folks like to classify as exogenous variables. Some of these are: I can't deal with the incompetents they keep sending me (translate: my training plan ain't what it ought to be); the people who determine these standards for service don't know anything about the problems of implementing social programs (translate: my ability to input field talent into determining standards *before* the fact is faulty); the whole thing is run by the legislature, there's just no logic to it at all (translate: as a political planner, I'm pretty much a bust); just when we learn how to do it their way, they change the requirements (translate: I need a plan to help my staff accommodate change.

Most of the variables we classify as exogenous turn out to be an integral part of the governmental process, terribly disconcerting if we play "Gee, Ain't It Awful," but highly manageable if we define the operational problem they create and plan for its treatment or elimination. Of course, playing "Gee Ain't It Awful" with a high powered governmental bunch is lots of fun (especially with enough scotch).

151

A few years ago, some people in Durham, North Carolina organized a company called M.I.C.A. (Management Improvement Corporation of America). Their business is helping governments do their business better. M.I.C.A. rarely gets involved in programs per se. Rather, its focus is on how programs get implemented. M.I.C.A. has flourished. One of the most interesting things about M.I.C.A. is that its fee is based on what its solutions save the governments for whom it works. The other interesting thing about M.I.C.A. is its own long-range plan. The founders of the company were mostly previous government officials. The long-range plan for M.I.C.A. is based on two premises. One is that implementing government programs is harder than thinking them up; the other is that most governments have no long-range plan for implementation. M.I.C.A.'s niche is helping governments carry out their plans—nuts and bolts implementation. Its success, particularly given the way it charges, seems to bear out the validity of M.I.C.A.'s long-range planning. People love them! They have lots of humpability, too!

CONTINGENCY PLANNING

The Sky Is Falling

Even the best gamblers have runs of bad luck. In the old movies, the Las Vegas visitor always saved bus fare home, and in college we always put aside enough for a couple of beers the first of each month when the G.I. checks came and we began our usual week-long poker game. Contingency planning is nothing more than long-range planning in the face of possible, or strongly suspected, or of known future events in the environment. In contingency planning, our forecast of the environment is considerably more certain. We assume that we know *what's* going to happen. What we don't know is *when*. So contingency planning formulates responses to possible events in advance of their occurrence. Then, when the "event" happens, we are ready with a carefully thought out response strategy, instead of being taken by surprise and forced to respond in haste. Contingency planning seeks to eliminate random responses to critical situations.

Exit signs in red, with suggestions that you familiarize yourself with the floor plan of your hotel before you retire, are a simple example of contingency planning. Management hopes that the hotel makes it through the night, but, in the event it doesn't, management doesn't want you wandering around the halls in your underwear looking for the doors; therefore, you are asked to do a bit of simple contingency planning. Civil defense planning is another example of contingency planning, in this case planning for an event to which we hope we can continue to attach miniscule probabilities. A very important type of contingency planning is built into our Constitution, for exam-

CONTINGENCY PLAN

ple, the orderly succession of power in the event of the unexpected demise of the president or even of his successor, the vice president. Estate planning is perhaps the most popular form of contingency planning. In this instance, the event (our eventual demise) is certain; but, because the time of that event cannot be predicted, we formulate (and revise) estate plans to provide for an orderly distribution of what we've managed to accumulate. My good friend Arthur DeBerry, the North Carolina general agent for a large insurance company, reminds me each month to give some thought to my "contingency" planning (his euphemism) with a grisly publication that he mails to me headlining the fact that estate taxes took an egregiously high percentage of Jack Benny's lifetime earnings, for example.

Into Each Life Some Rain
Must Fall

My friend Tom Triplett of Chester, South Carolina is a bridge contractor. Now that's nothing by itself; there are probably 200 of them around. But Tom is something special. He can build a bridge less expensively than anybody else. And make no mistake, his quality is as good as anybody's. Other contractors who have to bid against him cringe. How does he do it? Tom is a believer in planning, and he is a master at contingency planning. Have you ever driven by a bridge construction site on a rainy morning at 8 A.M. and watched 40 men stand around (my behavioral friends call this a milling exercise) waiting for some foreman to decide whether to go to work or go home? Forty men at ten bucks an hour all *milling*. Fantastic! Tom thinks that's nonsense. He has a well-thought-out contingency plan for every rainy day, and his contingency planning is so good that it really doesn't matter whether it rains at 8:00 A.M., 11:15 A.M., 3:07 P.M., or 4:42 P.M.

At each of his construction sites, you will find an old nondescript-looking semitrailer. But look inside and you'll find it air conditioned, with classroom seats for the whole bridge crew. You got it—an on-site classroom. Tom figures that instead of paying for "milling," he'd rather pay for education. So when it rains, the whole crew moves automatically indoors to go to school. There they are taught principles of management, bridge building, rigging, concrete forming, reinforcing wire tying—all the stuff that makes or breaks a contractor. Tom has an entire set of learning books covering all the normal bridge building trade skills. And here's the clincher: if you work for Tom as a laborer and if you have completed Tom's course for, say, rigger (a couple bucks an hour more pay), you just go to your foreman, ask him to give you the exam, and if you pass it, you *are* a rigger. Fantastic, you say. But think. Kings were fond of knighting men on the battlefield for superlative skill in battle; and General Curtis LeMay as head of the Strategic Air Command made lots of promotions at the foot of the ramp of his airplane; and look what Sir Walter Raleigh got for just one dirty coat. Lots of folks in the construction industry think Tom is a nut. But others who know him see him as the brightest light to come along in years. Those who compete against him wonder how in the hell he does it—with mirrors?

Harlan County, Kentucky

Many contingency plans focus on events significantly more consequential to the organization than rain. These are often called "doomsday" plans. I've been helping a large coal mining company in Harlan County, Kentucky lately; and I've come to have enormous respect for what they do, for the conditions under which they do it, and for the president of the company, Norman Yarborough. In an occupation as risky as coal mining, from time to time the dice do come up "craps." Norman has dedicated much of his life to safety in the mines. (He was awarded an honorary degree recently for his safety accomplishments on behalf of the miners.) Norman is a great believer in contingency planning. In his words, it comes out this way. Directly after a mine disaster is a damn poor time to plan what you'll do. So, at each of Norman's four mines, there is a safety team. The team spends quite a bit of time each month rehearsing what it will do under a wide variety of assumed disasters. Norman even holds an annual competition among the teams with the "disaster" unknown in advance. They practice, and practice, and practice—all on company time, and all to hone their responses to a hundred different disaster situations. Small wonder Norman's safety record is exemplary.

Everybody Does It

Much of military planning is the doomsday variety. In fact, the entire Strategic Air Command and ballistic missile organization operates (we trust) under a contingency plan that will never need to be implemented. Doomsdays are not always absolutely final, however. The eventual loss through retirement of a very successful company president is a kind of corporate doomsday—but of course not fatal, unless it happens without a carefully implemented contingency plan. Family succession in smaller companies is equally important. Here, however, the contingency plan becomes heavily embroiled in personalities, sibling rivalries, and a whole gamut of family pathologies—yet another reason for doing it instead of avoiding it. Finally, if you reflect for a moment on the amount of money reputedly on deposit in numbered Swiss bank accounts, you get some idea of the extent to which a variety of influential people around the world view contingency planning as a worthwhile endeavor.

But Overdoses Are Harmful

One of the greatest dangers of contingency planning is the tendency to rely on a dated action plan instead of on flexible current human judgment when the contingency arises. Take the red fire signs for instance. This year there was a fire at a

Holiday Inn in Ohio, at which it was nearly impossible for anyone to exit from the motel without breaking heavy glass windows in their rooms and jumping. The contingency plan for evacuation said nothing about breaking out your room window with your chair; it suggested instead that you find the red exit sign.

One must be very careful in prescribing future action by carefully drawn contingency plans, especially when you expect to have smart people at the helm. Look at the whaling ships operating out of New Bedford, Massachusetts during the last century. They were gone from their home port for three years or so without formal communication between owner and captain, and during that period the ship was expected to encounter *many* emergency situations. Yet (at least in all the movies) the departures from New Bedford ended with the wives and sweethearts on the dock all crying and waving hankies and the owner with his hand on the captain's shoulder saying, "Bring her back safely, John." Some contingency plan! Further examination indicates, however, that the contingency plan for that voyage was 20 years in the making, that is, the average time it took a bright, strong, apprentice lad to become a captain by understudying ten or so other captains as each of them faced a hundred emergencies successfully. (Oh what the telephone has done to self-reliance!)

Sizing up Again

Successful contingency plans always assess, first, how *critical* are the future events being planned for and, then, how much *time* the organization will have to respond through formal channels. And they evaluate the *ability* of the management to respond in that time frame. If the time will likely be very short and the ability of management in question, then the contingency plan is appropriately formal and detailed. On the other hand, if the ship will be out of port for three years and you have Gregory Peck at the helm, hell, give him a pat on the shoulder and tell him to "bring her back safely, John!"

We've already noted the caveat that substituting a highly detailed formal contingency plan for flexible current human judgment has risk. This risk is magnified when the formal contingency plan goes without revision for long periods of time. The value of recent information (and especially recent *local* information) has always been a prime ingredient in good decisions, and outdated contingency plans deny new information. A word to the wise should suffice. As a nineteenth-century New York investment banker, it would have been poor form to send your representative West with the admonition "do nothing till you hear from me by letter." The Pony Express guys were all good guys, true, but there were just too many Indians!

LONG-RANGE PLANNING FOR
NEW VENTURES

Heresy, You Say!

Bah humbug, entrepreneurs doing long-range planning—ruins the whole image of our cowboy capitalists. I thought entrepreneurs were supposed to ride their white horses fearlessly into the sunset (short run, of course) with little thought of what the long run would bring. Doesn't the enormous uncertainty associated with new ventures, only one in ten of which actually survives, make long-range planning a sort of managerial non sequitur? For the answers to these and other questions, stay tuned.

A Better Mousetrap

Einstein was attending a scientific meeting at which a colleague reported that he always carried a small notebook so that he could jot down good ideas as they came to him. The colleague suggested that it would be useful for Einstein to follow that practice too. The great scientist replied that it would be useless, because he had had only one good idea in his life. Successful entrepreneurial ventures don't generally result from short-run inspiration or a product idea that appears as did Abou Ben Adhem's angel in the middle of the night. Despite the success of Jim and Bob in Chapter 4, this kind of inside–out approach wins considerably less frequently than one that begins with a look *outside* at the market and its needs. And looking outside at the environment is a part of long-range planning, not of meditation while burning incense.

For years I prided myself on being able to evaluate mousetraps. I successfully identified (and helped exploit) better mousetraps in consulting, manufacturing, publishing, real estate, and agriculture—some fairly consequential ventures. Then one day about ten years ago an undergraduate business student named Roy (he wasn't even in my class) came to me with an idea for another fast-food restaurant in Chapel Hill (then there were only 50 or so). Roy told me that he had over $500 saved up to finance this deal and that he had been extraordinarily clever in renting this great building cheap (it turned out that this "great building" was two blocks off the beaten track). I listened for 15 minutes and then told Roy that I had 50 or 60 faster ways to lose money I'd let him have for nothing. Roy has not only survived these ten years—he has made a financial success of his venture. Roy's competitive advantage was staying open all night, providing a place for cops, drunks, insomniacs, partiers, term-paper writers, and other night people to congregate. And it turned out there wasn't another one of those in town. His place was so atmospheric (read, funky) that it got written up in a local literary magazine. He's fixed the place up, expanded it, and a few years ago he even bought this "great building." Roy is a real gentleman; he never reminds me of my mistake.

Needed: One Trash Sweeper

Entrepreneurs are not typically your better long-range planners; actually they're lousy planners. Entrepreneurs are doers. They're people of action, people who move impetuously at times, people who don't go wild over financial pro formas and market analyses—and, in general, people who pay little attention to the organization and *form* of their venture but lavish time and attention on the *idea* and its potential. My good friend Ritchie is one of these. Ritchie went to his banker about five years ago to borrow $75,000 to open up a bicycle shop. Ritchie explained in about three minutes that he could buy these bicycles for $80 and retail them for $170 and that, because he planned to sell 500 the first year and keep expenses to $20,000, he would make $25,000. He then asked the banker if he could have the check for $75,000. "Wait a minute, Ritchie," the banker said. "Where are your pro formas?" "Pro what?" said Ritchie, himself a botanist by trade. "Financial projections," the banker said. "We don't make any business loans without financials." Ritchie dropped by my office that afternoon dejected. "What is all this pro forma stuff?" he asked me. "Well," I said, "it's really not heavy stuff. Why don't you sit down for five minutes." I had a Portacom computer terminal under my desk and in about a minute I had dialed into our local time-sharing service and called up a pro forma statement generator program I wrote some years ago called PROFO. "Now Ritchie," I said, "how many of these do you intend to sell the first year?" "500." "And at what price?" "$170." "And what will they cost you?" "$80." To make a long story short, in five minutes my terminal had typed out a beautiful two-page pro forma income statement, balance sheet, and cash budget (by quarter no less). Ritchie went back down to the bank the next morning and had his $75,000 in one week. There are two hypotheses that can be tested from this anecdote. The first is that all good entrepreneurs need a trash sweeper type to sweep up the debris they leave behind as they move around, do the numbers, add a bit of long-range planning here and there, fend off creditors, inject a note of realism and objectivity into the whole process, and keep chaos out. The second hypothesis is that bankers really aren't as bright as most people think they are.

Becoming a successful entrepreneur is like running a maze quickly. You have to make the right turns at the right time to succeed. Some of these turns in entrepreneurship are critical, and making them at the right time calls for more than "back of old envelopes" planning.

In the first place, you must be assured of enough start-up capital to get things rolling, and it's a fact the financial folks really don't beat a path to your door to finance new ideas. You have to find start-up money the best way you can, from family and friends—you know, beg, borrow, or steal. And even friends like to see some figures. Second, by the time your start-up money is used up, you need to have your idea in good enough shape to show to the people who put up second-stage money. And these people like to see one of what you've got (preferably one that works) and lots and lots of pro formas (not the five-minute variety either).

And, then if you get stage 2 money, you've got to worry about getting the idea into production, which means all kinds of formalism: hiring people; making financial plans, budgets, cash flows; setting up production schedules—all the kind of stuff that needs a trash sweeper and more long-range planning. And, if you make it through this part of the maze, you begin to think about the big time, that's right, going public. And then long-range planning really pays off. All our current research on the new venture market bears out the fact that like Haley's Comet it appears only once in a while. The mid- to late-1960s was a terrific new ventures market, but in 1971 it dried up, and in 1976 there were only six new issues for the *whole year*. Hitting a gusher in the old Clark Gable oil wildcatter movies was a whole lot simpler than "cashing in" by going public with a new venture. You have to plan to be ready to move when the new issues window is open. And, if this isn't enough bad news, most entrepreneurs don't cash in personally on the primary new issue. They have to wait till the secondary public issue a few years later, which means more long-range planning to make sure things work out the way investors think they should. God knows, it's simpler to be a banker.

The smartest MBA I ever had in 20 years was Bill. Bill has made himself well-off financially and happy too as a very successful entrepreneur but of a particular variety, the "planning specie." Bill is a civil engineer by training, a man with an acute feel for figures—financials, pro formas, the whole gamut of planning devices that send first-year MBAs into wild delirium. But first and foremost Bill is an entrepreneur. He loves to work hard for himself and see results. Bill founded a mortgage insurance company in 1974 and went public at the founding. This is kind of like climbing Mt. Everest with a caravan of blind elephants during the monsoons. And he pulled it off. Bill is exceptionally bright, scrupulously honest, and immensely likeable and is one of the very few entrepreneurs I know today who really has a feel for and an appreciation of "trash sweeping." He not only understands what his trash sweepers do, he can do it better than they can. (He was also a hell of a football player for Duke University.) So the outcome isn't exactly a surprise, and it couldn't have happened to a better all-round planner/entrepreneur. Bill sold his company this year for $31.3 million. Bill has a great deal of humpability!

Sweat Capital
Dries up Too

All during this time that you've been practicing entrepreneurial frugality and "humpability" (running lean, leasing everything, working 14 hours a day, not seeing your spouse and kids for weeks, getting one person to do three jobs, stretching a dollar of working capital beyond the limit— "building a base" as the Big Eight accountants like to call it), you are stretching human resources mighty thin. The pressure for profits and survival makes it impossible for you to "staff up" like you want to, so you use sweat capital to keep the whole thing going. Now the trick with sweat capital is to balance it off with the present value of the pot of gold (going public or selling out for big bucks). You know, telling the troops (as they're dropping in their tracks) that success is just around the corner (or, as President Johnson was fond of saying about the war in Vietnam, there is light at the end of the tunnel). But each time that you have to put off the pot of gold another six months into the future, its present value gets smaller—at *any* discount rate—while today's sweat stinks just as much. This is the real juggling act of the successful entrepreneur.

Moral: Doing it successfully—pulling the whole deal off—takes some formal long-range planning; not the AT&T variety, of course, but not the "backs of old envelopes" kind either. It's rough to admit it, but entrepreneurship has gone uptown too!

INFLATION AND LONG-RANGE PLANNING

Running in Place

Inflation is everywhere, as much with us as McDonald's hamburgers, and there is no sign that its long-run cure is in sight. After years of examining long-range plans, I recently began asking people to have their planning or accounting staff deflate the figures in the plan either from single-year dollars to constant-year dollars, or, if the company situation permits, from dollars to units. Only in this way can I get any sense of whether we are moving ahead or merely jogging in place. This is not a unique approach; it's simply the only way I know to survive in the planning business.

Numbers have both a great impartiality about them and a great implied validity. If you read that General Motors' car sales increased by 8 percent, (1) you tend to believe it and (2) you get a sense of progress, of moving forward. If you are a stockholder, the gain is good news. If you are an employee, higher wages may be in sight. And, if you are just an ordinary person on the street, it's clear that G.M. is doing what all good companies ought to do—moving on, making more, getting bigger. Ah, but was it the car sales or the number of cars that increased 8 percent? It makes a hell of a difference. In an economy inflating at 10 percent, an 8 percent increase in dollar car sales translates to a 2 percent reduction in the number of cars built (assuming of course that inflation takes its proportionate toll on the auto industry and that model size mix stays about like it was). Now this gives us a different picture: things are worse, we're going backward, production is falling, the dream is coming apart. Not only is the picture altered for stockholders, employees, and persons on the street, but it is altered for company management as well. If inflation can change the signals this drastically, it *must* be factored into the long-range planning process. Inflation doesn't hide double faults in tennis, bogies in golf, or losses at poker—nor should it be allowed either to camouflage real performance in an organization. The consequences of inflated signals are too expensive.

Always Count in Units

Units of output and dollars of output mean entirely different things to production executives. More units take more machines and more facilities to produce and vice versa, whereas more dollars *may* take fewer machines and less space depending on the inflation rate. Likewise, inventories of more units take more physical space to store and vice versa, but inventories worth more dollars *may* require more or less space depending on inflation. Manpower planning in most organizations is done in standard minutes or standard hours of production time per unit. But inflation affects this area too. It's quite possible to produce more dollars of output with fewer persons while productivity falls simultaneously—you can easily work out the dismal inflation rates that would do it for your company. Conversely, it is nearly impossible to increase unit output while productivity decreases (unless you do it with mirrors). Conclusion: Long-range production planning in dollars is dangerous. Always count in units.

Always Count in Dollars

Financial types like to think in dollars. Units are messy, have grease on them, and get your three-piece suit dirty. More dollars of production, more dollars in inventory, and more dollars in receivables take more dollars of working capital, which means that you have to borrow more dollars or appeal to equity holders for more dollars, which means you get to use your three-piece suit. But, if sales forecasts for the planning horizon are constant in units, capital requirements *still* rise in an inflating economy. Good for using your three-piece suit, but hard to explain to some bankers who wonder why "it takes more to make less" keeps coming out. Knocks the hell out of their Robert Morris ratio mindsets. Conclusion: Using unit sales figures for financial planning is dangerous. Always count in dollars.

*Always Count
Everything—Selectively*

Marketing types like to count everything (everything that's going up, that is), anything to make nice colored lines with positive slopes for wall charts or slides. If unit sales are sliding in a highly inflationary economy, they can look good measuring dollars. If unit sales are going up madly during a tame inflation period, for heaven's sake, let them measure unit sales then—makes for great marketing planning, knowing exactly what's happening! Conclusion: We've been unfair to marketing types. Most of them really care, some of them understand, a few of them can count.

Always Count
Everything—It's Safer

Accounting types have always been characterized as the most risk averse in the corporate henhouse. Theoretically, then, it should be easy to convince them that both unit and dollar figures (or at least good deflated dollar figures) have an uncontested place as inputs in corporate strategic planning. In fact, a number of companies today are using inflation accounting techniques for external reporting. What is clearly needed, however, is greater use of inflation accounting data in long-range planning, in supportive facilities and financial planning, and in the shorter-run comparative budgetary analysis. Conclusion: All accountants can count, most of them care, many of them understand, but few of them can explain it.

Why Worry
At All?

Although indexing as a remedy for inflation has had some limited success in a few Latin American countries, it is not the solution to long-range planning in an inflationary economy. Inflation must be recognized and counted. Long-range planning agendas dealing with forecasts must know how these translate into appropriate actions for today, and, without factoring in inflation assumptions, this is nearly impossible. Conclusion: It is a corporate sin of omission to let the lack of thinking about what to count screw up a good plan.

LONG-RANGE PLANNING FOR
YOUR CAREER

Sense versus Nonsense

Lots of successful executives will tell you that getting ahead is a process of working your tail off and staying out of trouble. That is pure *nonsense*. Getting ahead in an organization is a careful process of (1) having enough "stuff" (ability, humpability, intelligence, personality, etc.) and (2) careful implementation of the right long-range career plan. A long-range career plan is focused on such considerations as (1) making sure that you are in the right place given your abilities; (2) making sure you have sized up yourself, the competition, and the available job opportunities correctly and objectively; (3) being sufficiently visible to those in positions of power in your organization; (4) examining your boss's present and future impact on your long-range career plan; (5) identifying constraints to desired upward movement—"the gap"; (6) laying out alternatives for removing the gap; (7) getting enough support when it's time to make your move; and (8) making certain that you recognize the trade-offs implicit in your long-range career plan and that these are congruent with your lifestyle, family style, and personal style.

But, you ask, what does the management development director do? Careful here—it's true that many organizations do have management development systems, but only a fool leaves formal career planning to this system. After all, it's still true that the good Lord helps those who help themselves, and it was never truer than in long-range career planning. The formal system makes sure (at least pro forma) that you have enough stuff to get in the door; it places you in your first position where the organization needs your help; it ensures that you receive job performance reviews at carefully stipulated intervals; it ensures that you get the right kind of training from time to time; it makes sure that you have not been discriminated against on the basis of race, creed, color, religion, or national origin; and it dutifully and methodically records all this (as well as any indiscretions along the way) in your personnel file. But it just doesn't do long-range career planning, that is, help you set and reach your goals. Not convinced? OK, go back and take another look at those eight items just enumerated. Which one of those does the formal management development plan in your organization accomplish? None! Fact: You've got to do it yourself!

Sizing Everybody Up—
Including You

In Chapter 3, we examined how organizations size themselves up prior to looking at strategic alternatives. In the same sense that they probe themselves to find out where they are tough and where they are weak, so must you go through the same process. Without it, you cannot identify job responsibilities that are properly matched with your abilities, you cannot evaluate the competition, and you cannot get a sense of what you need to do to remove a personal gap if one exists. One of the best ways to get yourself sized up is by noncompeting peers, that is, by people of about your own age and career status who do *not* work for the same organization (and who thus can afford to be brutally honest, which is exactly what you need at this point). And an excellent place to find a smart bunch like this is at an executive training conference (off corporate campus, of course). After a week or two with, say, 40 people like yourself, if you're smart enough to use out-of-class time wisely, you can get a strong sense of where you are in the pack. It's a lot like leaving high school where you were a big local dog and finding out when you get to the university that you're just another number down in the second quartile. Makes for some site readjustments—salutary stuff in long-range career planning.

Ask your spouse to size you up; spouses are great sources for sizing-up help. Although your spouse may not be familiar with your corporate behavior, or with the demands of various alternative career paths, he or she is very familiar with your general ability, your personality, and your humpability. And that assessment given honestly and objectively is worth plenty! You can use your boss to size you up too, but be careful here. It's one thing to get "career improvement" advice of a general nature from your boss, but it's completely different (and risky as hell) to dwell with him at great length on your personal deficiencies that you know more about than he. Something about sleeping dogs, I believe! Don't forget good friends too— particularly the kind that will tell you that you are a smart cookie and a good friend and that they love you, but that at times they just don't *like* some of the things you do. You need to find out those "things" fast!

And don't forget your company peers. There are plenty of occasions to see them and you in action together—meetings, lunches, trips, presentations. Ask yourself what they are good at, what they are better at than you, what you are better at than they, how you present yourself, whether you do well with questions extemporaneously, whether you're as articulate as they (both oral and written form are important), and a hundred other relevant comparisons that, taken together, will give you a good sense of just how tough you are. There is no other way; you simply have to compare. It's like fishing. I think I'm a good fisherman, my wife thinks I'm a good fisherman, and I *am* a good fisherman. That is, until I fish with good fishermen!

Sizing-up involves too a kind of personal assessment that only you can do. Of all the people who know you, you are probably the best qualified to answer such questions as what things have I done in this company that turned me on, what kinds of organizational responsibilities here have turned me off, what kind of person do I do well under, what kind of boss do I abhor working for, what experiences would I gladly repeat, and which ones would cause me to quit? These very personal sizing-up questions are often difficult to face. It's always tempting to assume that you will be smart enough to change to face *whatever* organizational situations face you. But my psychologist friends tell me that, if you're over 14 years old, changing yourself radically is nonsense too. (Or maybe they said age 6.)

Finally, you have to face the hardest part of the long-range career plan size-up, your *life-style*. What will you trade off for what? Will you trade family for promotion, children for position, spouse for career movement, family stability for geographical moves, personal freedom for rewarded conformity? Every one of these is a critical part of sizing-up. If you haven't faced a hard choice yet, these may sound like artificial dilemmas. They're *real*. An honest answer to each one of these questions goes a long way in the implementation of sensible long-range career planning, but honest it must be. But, you say, there's time for the spouse and children later; first, we'll make these absolutely critical career supporting moves, then we'll worry about the family. We'll invest 10 to 15 years in this career alternative to make enough money to take care of us for the rest of our lives. Now come on, you don't have to be a psychologist to know that behavior is age–appropriate. The world looks askance at a 60-year-old trying to relive something he or she missed at 14. And it's a certainty that time cannot be inventoried for use later at *any* cost! That's precisely why this part of the long-range career planning size-up is critical. You can't have it all, so decide what you want, what you want the *most,* and what you can live without to get what you really want without messing up any lives—your own or others!

Objectives, Horatio Alger,
And Laurence J. Peter

Where do you want to go from here? When people ask you that, what do you say? Too many people respond with "to the top, of course," as if that were the optimum. Nonsense again! Laurence J. Peter's interesting book, *The Peter Princi-*

ple, should have been enough to dissuade intelligent executives from overextending as a career strategy; unfortunately, too many still do. Reaching for the stars is an old American tradition, Horatio Alger and all that. Dreaming the big dream, making a million, going for the top—all these goals are on the side of the angels; they all get high marks for ambition, but they may in fact flunk the test of objectivity. If your size-up shows you to be only average in the qualities requisite to go to the top in your organization, and if the competition is tough, how are you supposed to get there? Only two ways, luck and hard work. Now we've all read the folklore about major corporation presidents who were just average but who worked their fannies off. That's good for career-day talks at the local high school but hardly the stuff good long-range career planning is made of. (And, if your career plan is founded solely on being lucky, then you and I have a serious matter we need to chat about sometime.)

The key is not going to *the* top, it's going to *your* top. If you get to your top and still feel tough, and if Dame Fortune smiles at you unexpectedly one day, then try for the moon. But as Peter implies, don't reach for the moon in your organization (the presidency) if you have just enough stuff for a functional vice presidency. There is no terror and no anxiety equal to playing out of your league with simultaneous pressure from top, bottom, and home. That's the stuff that keeps the Valium plant on overtime. A good match of what you have and what the position demands, that's the career objective that keeps people happy—and sane too.

Bosses

My boss is a great guy, I work for a very bright woman, my boss is a fair guy, my boss is a nice person, my boss likes me—all irrelevant! The relevant issue for long-range career planning is not whether your boss is great, bright, fair, nice, or likes you but whether he or she can help you attain your career objective. Your boss either helps you or hurts you. Bosses *seldom* play neutral roles in the advancement of subordinates. Now which is it? Is your boss helping or hurting your career plans? How can you tell? It's really not all that difficult. Is your boss well connected to the power in the organization (the folks that make the whole thing go)? Do you trust your boss? Is your boss consulted on consequential matters around here? Has your boss been passed over for promotion lately? Does your boss have "organizational visibility"? Has your boss held the same position for more than five years? Is your boss considered to be on the "fast track" around the organization? Has your boss ever taken credit for one of your accomplishments? If the answer to any of these questions bothers you, then you're beginning to see that bosses cannot be considered neutral; they either help or hurt your career.

Don't forget these behaviors can be *sub rosa* too, with such style that it's often hard for subordinates to recognize what's happening. I attended an organizational strategy meeting for a bank earlier this summer. One of my brightest MBAs works for them, and she's a real winner. Brighter than her boss and ready for a move up. Her boss was questioned by the bank president about Ellen's qualifications for promotion to a position almost as high as the one that her boss held—all this in an open meeting. Her boss responded with, "Ellen's a terrific woman. In about two more years, she'll be ready for that job. In fact, she'll be great for it, but she's not quite ready today." Her boss got lots of "atta boys" from the group for recognizing talent, for nurturing talent, for being concerned with the development of his subordinates, and for not exposing the organization to a woman who is "not quite ready." In point of fact, he set back Ellen's long-range career plan by exactly two years! She keeps his job for him by the quality and volume of *her* work. See how nicely it works? Once again with feeling: Your boss is either helping or hurting your chances to reach your objective.

My Worst Fears

So he's hurting you, don't panic. There are three simple courses of action in this case. You can stay. (Be sure to figure up how many years till your boss retires, if you choose this path.)

You can get yourself transferred within the same organization. Or you can quit. If time is against waiting it out (if your boss just has too many more years to go), you are down to two choices very quickly. If you have some built-up personal equity in the organization, then you want to stay there if you can; if not, quitting may be a good play at this time. Remember, though, that the "quitting game" can be played only a limited number of times. After your quota of quits, you're known as a "talented malcontent," and nobody loves you anymore. Nevertheless, when that's the thing to do, don't be bashful—quit!

Getting transferred can be done in two ways: either make it worthwhile for your boss to turn you out (nearly impossible if you are keeping your boss alive by your work and not clever enough to slack off so he'll get rid of you) or get yourself "adopted." Getting yourself adopted is greatly preferred. To do this you must create more visibility for yourself, but visibility with a focus. What you're trying to do is get someone with enough organizational clout to adopt you away from your boss. You can create visibility by making a stunning presentation at a meeting where your intended foster parent sees you, or by judicious use of copies of reports and memos that you have written, or by shrewdly letting it be known (in a fairly limited circle, please) that you *can* be adopted and that you don't eat much (i.e., your work output is high, very high). Or, if you have the guts for it, you can make a direct frontal approach to the person you want to work for. This last alternative is quick, but in the best tradition of no free lunch in America it is *very* risky. In sum, if your boss is hurting your career, you must get out. How you do it is strictly tactics.

Odds and Ends
in Organizations

Item: All executives make "deals" with their bosses, deals about when they'll get promoted, what they'll be doing a year from today, when they'll get his job, and the like. This is normal but incomplete organizational behavior. An intelligent subordinate realizes as a part of his long-range career planning

173

process that bosses come and go. Therefore, to preserve the validity of deals that are made, he needs to make certain that the boss's boss knows about the deals between him and his boss—at least the important ones. Moral: Go ye and do likewise.

Item: You don't get ahead in an organization by putting the competition down. *First,* that hurts everybody (you included), and you come off as a poor mouther, a bad handle to have. *Second,* you never know when you'll be working for the competition. Elephants are not the only creatures with long memories. *Third,* it's hard to generate loyalty from your staff when they see you putting someone else down. But, most important, trying to get ahead by putting down the competition gives a bad name to an otherwise interesting and reasonably fair game—getting ahead.

Item: Visibility is vital in executive long-range career planning. Though it may sound crass to insist that you must be visible to the power in the organization, that's just the way it is. People in power who don't know you and are not aware of your capabilities can hardly help your career. Whenever you get a chance to appear before the higher ups, look brilliant! When you draft a memo or letter that will be seen by people in power, make it brilliant too. And make sure that the chief executive of your organization knows you by name. Whenever you see him and he can't seem to remember your name, for God's sake, help him; make it easy for the chief executive in a meeting of the executive committee to suggest that Susan McGinty be considered strongly for that new job as vice president, instead of his sitting there and saying, "What's the name of that nice looking young redhead who works down in . . . where does she work?" Career differences often turn on much less than that.

Finally, in long-range career planning, remember that, as in corporate strategic long-range planning, it's a continuing process. Every time you get moved up, the process begins again. And, if you *don't* get moved up, that's a critical time in the process too. Time to reassess your chances, your "stuff," your objectives, and your boss. (You know, the good Lord helps those who help themselves.) Sitting around playing "Gee Ain't It Awful" don't feel too good, whereas getting what you want is a gas. And getting there—the long-range career planning process—is half the fun. Nuff said.

SEVEN

Sources of Long-Range Planning Information

All the numbers you really need ... and in one place too.

I have an unparalleled record of error in political forecasting. I never make predictions. They can only embarrass you. The other day I found a prediction that Milton Friedman made only five years ago, that OPEC could never raise oil to $10 a barrel.

John Kenneth Galbraith (1979)

OK, COACH, WE'VE HAD THE COURSE, NOW CAN WE GRADUATE?

Not yet. I've got one more play to show you. We've drilled the basics, steps 1 through 7, of the long-range planning process. This concluding chapter offers a few hints on facilitating a very tough step in the planning process—forecasting the environment. So back to step 4 for five minutes of advice, then—school's out!

Recall that steps 1, 2, and 3 consisted of gathering and processing information about our organization: its history (step 1), its toughness today (step 2), and its objectives (step 3). Let's assume that we have access to all the information we need on the internal environment, that is, on our own organization. The external environment is a lot tougher to assess. For step 4, we're seeking information on the world outside our door to forecast where it's going. We're looking at our industry, competitors, current markets, and untapped markets; the state of the art and impending technological change; government regulators and judicial and legislative trends—whatever is relevant in the outside world in which our organization operates.

Obviously the amount of potentially useful data is staggering. Equally as obvious, our resources are limited: only so much time and money. And what we're really interested in is the end product, the forecast. So what now, Coach?

178

*There are two ways to get a forecast: (1)
do it yourself or (2) pay a professional
forecaster to do it.*

Start by considering both alternatives. You might have the time, money, and competence to do it all by yourself. Or you might want to forecast in the area you're familiar with, say, technological changes in your industry, and go to an outside expert for a forecast of a particular problem, say, future costs of government regulation. Or you could hire a big-name outfit to put the whole thing in a neat (possibly expensive) package—like Chase Econometrics or Arthur D. Little. (The level of sophistication for hire can be incredibly high; witness the Wharton Econometric Model with 1,800 variables that can solve for 35 countries simultaneously—available for about $9,500—1979 price.) Alternatively, you might find a good local or regional consulting group to sell you the whole forecast.

I personally am a firm believer in managers' doing for themselves—but only up to the limits of their training and ability. You have to be a smart executive to recognize the point at which you're about to exceed your competence in ciphering a particularly difficult forecast and need to call in expert help. But, if you have the judgment to send for reinforcements when needed, go on and do your forecasting in-house, and more power to you!

This chapter concludes with a list of information sources for forecasting, among which are the names of several prominent research and forecasting organizations. Some of the biggies have services that a small to medium-sized company could use (others probably not—our list is meant to show you what's there, not to make specific recommendations). The remainder of this chapter suggests where and how to gather useful data for making forecasts. (Forecasting *techniques* are adequately described in a number of textbooks on the market.)

*What is the answer? [Silence] In that case,
what is the question?*

Gertrude Stein

Your search for forecast data should begin with the
question, "What do I want to know?" *not* "I think I'll go read up
on Nigeria." State what you're looking for at the beginning;
this will conserve time, money, and your good temper. If you
know what you're looking for, you're better able to discriminate
what is useful. Frequently you'll find that there is too much information available rather than too little. In those instances,
raw data will bury you like an avalanche unless you know from
the start what data you're after. Then you nimbly extract it and
run like hell.

Sure it sounds obvious. But it's human nature to forget
to watch the ball. And that's what keeps batting coaches,
consultants, and authors in business—anyone who makes a
buck intoning, "Keep your eye on the ball, keep your eye on the
ball, keep your eye on the ball."

Have library card, will travel.

Consider hiring a gofer to dig up your information.
There are plenty of industrious graduate students, under-
employed spouses, and assorted moonlight researchers whose
time costs less than yours and who are good at getting information—leaving you more time for your real job, which is
analysis, that is, turning input into output. If you want to figure
out whether you can sell machine tools to China and, if so, how
many in 1995, you've got a lot of leg work ahead gathering information. Delegate, or hire somebody reliable, to do that part;

then you do the ciphering after they bring back the data. Makes sense. (I even have one former student, Mary Ellen Templeton, a professional librarian with an MBA degree, who has started her own company in Durham, N.C., Spectrum Information Services, to perform specialized information searches. Basically, her product is efficiency. She's an inside–out planner.)

D.L.'S
HELPFUL HINT NO. 4

> *"Good morning, Wilson Library Business Reference Section. This is the oracle speaking."*

Discover reference librarians. They are the modern inhabitants of the temple at Delphi. They know *everything* or else they know where to find·it. These wonderful professionals make their living looking up information for people like us, or guiding us around as we do it ourselves.

Ideally, ask a business reference librarian what you want to know; he or she will tell you where to look. Business reference librarians are specialists attached to university libraries. But any garden-variety reference librarian is just as good. These people delight in figuring out how to find anything out. Lucky for us.

D.L.'S
HELPFUL HINT NO. 5

> *Let your fingers do the walking.*
> Alexander Graham Bell

Use the phone. When you want to get information fast, or find the right person to ask, the phone is your best friend. You can even *call* business reference librarians (three blocks away or in the next state)—not to mention the U.S. Department of

Agriculture and that lady with the $5 forecast on Highway 301 between Selma and Four Oaks, North Carolina.

D.L.'S
HELPFUL HINT NO. 6

If there were just two guys in the world collecting and selling turkey buzzard eggs, you can be sure that one of the two would start a monthly Turkey Buzzard Egg Dealers Journal *and sell it to the other one.*

Trade journals are stuffed with facts and figures on nearly every industry. You're already familiar with the trade publications in your field—consider looking through the trade papers for any other industry you need to bone up on. *Women's Wear Daily, Nation's Restaurant News, World Wood, Professional Builder, Chronicle of Higher Education, Shopping Center World, Motor Inn Journal*—there are hundreds. For the price of your time (or your gofer's) plus a trip to the library (or a subscription), you can dig out info cheap that a consultant would charge dearly for. It just takes a little ingenuity, and maybe a reference librarian, to find the data on unfamiliar territory.

Corollary: The same goes for trade organizations. For example, the North Carolina Yam Commission, funded by the state's sweet potato growers, will tell you anything it knows about profitable uses of sweet potatoes, the latest techniques for storage, and the probable output of Johnston County— the biggest sweet-potato-producing county in the United States—for the next five years. I gave up counting the number of state associations for trades, businesses, professions, and special interest groups in the Raleigh, North Carolina phone book when I got to 56 and still had a page and a half of fine print to go. It's worth repeating: trade associations and trade journals are a goldmine of information. Dig where the digging's easy.

*What's black and white and read all over,
and comes in the next day's mail? (And I'm
not talking about what the Adam and Eve
company sells.)*

Look into the printed matter issued by the district office of the U.S. Department of Commerce in your state. All you have to do is find the liaison person and make friends, then call up anytime for help. Forty-four states in the U.S. have outposts of the U.S. Department of Commerce (not to be confused with the states' own commerce departments). They can help you extract the data you want from the reams and tons and rooms and mountains of statistics compiled by this agency of the U.S. government. May save you a trip to Washington. So check this source out.

LISTS
LISTS
LISTS

We've compiled a list for you (me and my gofers and some helpful reference librarians). These are information sources to get you started in your forecast data collecting. They are the best and most basic sources we could find in five categories. You probably already know where to look in your own field, be it furniture making, museum fund raising, or commuter air service. Here are some other sources. Our list has five sections, each arranged alphabetically: (1) general, (2) the economy, (3) international (cross-referenced to the other sections), (4) technology, (5) the future. It's still a bit of a grabbag; you'll find no- or low-cost sources side by side with very expensive ones—consulting groups, government publications, other lists, journals of planning—a little of everything. Skim the titles and check our comments; we've attempted to summarize the usefulness of each entry as well as the cost. These are just to get you started. Once you start using these sources, one is likely to lead you to another, and so on till you find exactly what you want.

(If you find excellent basic information sources not listed here, write me—I'd like to add them to my list.)

PARTING SHOT

I happen to know (from a friendly reference librarian) that it takes up to 1,500 tons of South African ore to yield one gold bar weighing 400 troy ounces. Getting that down to my buying power, up to 3.75 tons of ore are required to produce a single krugerrand, or 1 troy ounce. And that's one hell of a lot of blasting, digging, hauling, crushing, sifting, washing, melting, and refining between finding the raw stuff in the bowels of the earth and delivering 400 krugerrands to a New York gold dealer so that I can buy one on Tuesday morning. (My daughter Lisa says you've got to kiss a lot of toads to find one prince. Same idea.)

Sifting through statistics and other data is like mining gold ore. You have to dig up and then process a lot of it to yield any conclusions of value—3.75 tons of facts and numbers to yield an ounce of forecast, and all that mental effort and computer time in between. And, when you're done, you've still got steps 5 through 7 of the long-range planning process ahead of you. There must be easier ways to make a living. But remember the payoff: there's a pony in there somewhere, or a krugerrand, or a prince.

GENERAL

AMERICAN INSTITUTE OF PLANNERS
1776 Massachusetts Avenue, N.E.
Washington, D.C. 20036   (202) 872-0611

Journal of the American Institute of Planners has been published since 1925. It deals mainly with environmental and social issues.

ARTHUR D. LITTLE, INC.
25 Acorn Park
Cambridge, Massachusetts 02140

Arthur D. Little, Inc. is a well-known forecasting research and planning consultant group that forecasts 5 to 25 years into the future. The firm will do consulting work for a fee. (Big league.)

THE BOSTON CONSULTING GROUP, INC.
One Boston Place
Boston, Massachusetts 02106   (617) 722-7800

These people have a unique and fairly accurate method of helping business decide where (by product) their money can be best invested. They are sagacious long-range planners whose clients are generally of the multinational persuasion.

THE CONFERENCE BOARD
845 Third Avenue
New York, New York 10022   (212) 759-0900

A nonprofit, often-quoted, membership business research and education organization.

Although these people aren't the most helpful if you don't have money to spend, they do offer their publications to nonmembers for from $3.00 to $75.00. Areas of research focus on executive use and include business economics, general administration, finance, personnel administration, marketing, international operations management, and public affairs.

DANIELLS, LORNA
Baker Library
Harvard Business School
Boston, Massachusetts   (617) 495-6378

Forecasting in the Eighties is not yet published, but, as in her *Forecasting in the Seventies* (and *Sixties*) edition, she lists books and articles useful to business forecasters. It is an invaluable, highly recommended list. She is responsible for other publications regarding business information sources. All available from your guide, the reference librarian, or from the Harvard Business School publishers. Also *Business Reference Sources* (1971); *Business Literature: An Annotated List for Students and Businessmen;* and *Core Collections* (not by Lorna Daniells but available from the Harvard Business School).

> ### ENCYCLOPEDIA OF ASSOCIATIONS
> Co-edited by Nancy Yakes and Denise Akey
> 13th Edition
> Gale Research Company
> Book Tower
> Detroit, Michigan 48226

An unusual encyclopedia that purports to be the most comprehensive source of detailed information on American membership organizations. You can find any trade or other type of association in this book.

> ### LONG-RANGE PLANNING JOURNAL
> Published by Pergamon Press Ltd.
> Headington Hill Hall
> Oxford, England 64881

Long-Range Planning is a bimonthly publication that costs $66.00 per year. Its focus is on the concepts and techniques used by senior management, government administrators, and academies in developing strategy and long-range plans.

> ### MARKETING RESEARCH SERVICES, U.S.A
> Division of A.C. Nielsen Company
> International Headquarters
> Nielsen Plaza
> Northbrook, Illinois 60062   (404) 393-1010

Extensive and expensive market research.

NORTH AMERICAN SOCIETY OF CORPORATE PLANNERS (NASCP)
1406 Third National Building
Dayton, Ohio 45402   (513) 223-0419

Executive planning officers with a particular interest in planning the future. Holds monthly meetings with speakers.

STATE UNIVERSITIES

The economics, political science, or planning departments (to name a few) at your state university will not only have volumes of information on the future status of resources and economic trends but will probably also have a group of enthusiastic people who want to tell you everything they know. Write or call them. There is frequently a high level of competence there.

U.S. GOVERNMENT

When asked to give a list of government employees broken down by sex, the incumbent politician said, "Well, we've had a few alcoholics, but I don't believe any one of them has been broken down by sex."

Someone somewhere in the bowels of the bureaucracy knows the answer to every question, and also keeps every statistic ever discovered. (And they love to talk on the phone.) We give you the first phone number to try. Someone will refer you to someone. Eventually you'll get the right number.

U.S. DEPARTMENT OF AGRICULTURE
Washington, D.C.   (202) 655-4000

The major available information sources are in Economics, Statistics, and Cooperative Service; Foreign Agricultural Data; Daily Market Information; Food and Nutrition Information Center; Food Consumption Research Group; Technology; and Innovation.

U.S. DEPARTMENT OF COMMERCE
Washington, D.C.
(or your local state office)   (202) 377-2000

If you have never used their services or read their publications, hold on for the surprise of your life. They offer, for free or for a minimal charge, boundless information. Statistics on the production, export, and import of all products are available by SIC code (standard industrial classification). You can find out almost anything you need to know about domestic and foreign trade (but didn't know where to look).

Among the available services and publications are

1. *Foreign Economic Trends* (FET). The latest economic indicators for over 100 countries. Very readable.
2. *Overseas Business Reports* (OBR). Detailed marketing information, trade outlooks, statistics, regulations, and market profiles.
3. *Global Market Surveys* (GMS). Detailed information on 15 to 20 of the best foreign markets for a specific industry or group of related industries.
4. *International Economic Indicators.* Extensive comparative economic statistics for the U.S. and other foreign countries.
5. An index of *Selected Publications to Aid Business and Industry.*

The *Bureau of Census* is a part of the Commerce Department. You will get demographic, economic, industrial, and almost any other statistic you want from the Census Bureau.

DISTRICT OFFICES, U.S. DEPARTMENT OF COMMERCE

You will need a guide through the statistical thickets of Commerce and the Census. Fortunately, there are willing guides. Call the Industrial Division of the District Office, U.S. Department of Commerce, in your state and tell your "guide" what information you want. In North Carolina, you receive it the next day in the mail—and it's actually free. Available in 44 states.

DEPARTMENT OF LABOR
Washington, D.C.   (202) 655-4000

Information sources and material include the Bureau of Labor Statistics; national economic data; state, regional and local economic statistics; industry statistics; consumer expenditure studies; occupational safety and health statistics; labor–management information; international statistics.

DEPARTMENT OF STATE
Washington, D.C.   (202) 655-4000

Available material and sources include country background notes (synopses of political, historical, economic background of foreign countries); Agency for International Development; export opportunities.

DEPARTMENT OF TRANSPORTATION
Washington, D.C.   (202) 655-4000

The Department of Transportation has a Transportation Research Information System.

DEPARTMENT OF THE TREASURY
Washington, D.C.   (202) 566-2000

The Treasury Department could be one of the most helpful agencies of the government. There is an Office of Statistical Reports; Office of Gold Market Activities; Business Statistics; Corporate Statistics; Individual Statistics; Foreign and Wealth Statistics; Office of Tax Analysis; Bureau of Alcohol, Tobacco, and Firearms; Comptroller of the Currency.

HANDBOOK FOR BUSINESS ON USE
OF GOVERNMENT STATISTICS
Tayloe Murphy Institute
Box 6550
Charlottesville, Virginia 22906

This book could help you find the right numbers faster.

WASHINGTON RESEARCHERS
918-16th Street, N.W.
Washington, D.C. 20006   (202) 828-4800

They are a terrific source of information. Bimonthly *Information Reports* list addresses, telephone numbers, and types of information available and where to go to get it. Their "main expertise is in identifying little-known sources of information and presenting facts in an easy-to-understand format." Call them for a price quotation on a research project.

THE ECONOMY

Business will be better or worse.
Calvin Coolidge

THE BROOKINGS INSTITUTION
1775 Massachusetts Avenue, N.W.
Washington, D.C. 20036   (202) 797-6000

"Brookings, " as it is fondly called, is a policy-oriented research institute—a think tank—whose publications focus on the economy, government, foreign policy, and the social sciences. It is a friendly institution. You can write for its catalog of publications on sectors of the domestic or worldwide economy. For example, it has a publication called "Long-Term Growth of Output and Productivity" (in the U.S.). Brookings is an academic institution with a lot of credibility.

CHASE ECONOMETRIC ASSOCIATES, INC.
555 City Lane Avenue
Bala Cynwyd, Pennsylvania 19009

(New York telephone)   (212) 269-1188

This subsidiary of Chase Manhattan Bank provides consulting services to larger companies because, as one employee put it, "Small companies don't make long range plans . . . " but it will provide excellent service, including eight days consulting time, macroeconomic forecasts, building a model for the individual company to anticipate the market, and the like for $7,500–15,000 per year. It has a macro-service that gives an extensive report on one particular industry of your choice for $3,000; very competent, worth the money, but make sure it's for you.

COMMITTEE FOR ECONOMIC DEVELOPMENT
477 Madison Avenue
New York, New York 10022   (212) 688-2065

or

1000 Connecticut Avenue, N.W.
Washington, D.C. 20036   (202) 296-5860

The Committee for Economic Development is concerned about the economy. Some of its major projects include "Controlling for New Inflation," "Improving the Long-Term Performance of the U.S. Economy," and "Meeting the Needs for Adequate Capital." Write for reports for a fee. It is a private, nonprofit research center made up of 200 national business leaders.

DATA RESOURCES, INC. (DRI)
29 Hartwell Avenue
Lexington, Massachusetts 02173

(617) 861-0165

DRI has an econometric model of the U.S. It is the largest economic information bank in the world. It has over 5 million time series. DRI says that it is now developing services for small- to medium-sized companies. Its services include, but are not limited to, the following:

1. *Macroeconomic outlook: gives the GNP, interest and production rate, using 800–1000 variables in a monthly publication. For $16,000 a year you can have this and access to DRI data on your computer terminal.*
2. *Off-line services for information (hard copies of reports) for $5,000.*
3. *Special projects.*

Clients pay anywhere from $2,000 to $200,000 annually for DRI's services.

THE ECONOMIST
The Economist Newspaper Ltd.
25 St. James's Street
London, SWIA 1 HG, United Kingdom
(London telephone)   (01) 839-7000

Excellent weekly journal similar to *Business Week* but more precise and highly useful. Published in England. International focus.

PREDICASTS, INC.
200 University Circle Research Center
11001 Cedar Avenue
Cleveland, Ohio 44106   (216) 795-3000

Predicasts is an invaluable resource. Competent people. Predicasts believes in letting you decipher the information. Three main sources are available.

1. Prompt: *A digest of articles from 2,500 publications by SIC codes ($675 per year). Continually updated.*
2. F&S Index: *Index of periodical articles (foreign and domestic). Found in most libraries.*
3. Predicasts to 1990: *Statistical quarterly of present and future trends, by SIC code ($475 per year).*

Note: You can also hook up to their computer ($2,000), have industry studies done of past and future trends ($625), and attend two-day monthly seminars on use of Predicast's information computer access, held all over the U.S. for $60 per person.

STANFORD RESEARCH INSTITUTE,
BUSINESS INTELLIGENCE PROGRAM
333 Ravenswood Avenue
Menlo Park, California 94025   (415) 326-6200

This program studies the business world and reports on economic, social, political, or technological changes. Its monthly publication, *Datalog,* has published the following studies: "Handbook of Forecasting Techniques" and "Industrial Automation in Discrete Manufacture." Stanford consults, conducts seminars, and does special information searches. Write to see if it has what you want.

WHARTON ECONOMICS FORECASTING
ASSOCIATES, INC.
One University City
4025 Chestnut Street
Philadelphia, Pennsylvania 19104
                              (215) 243-6451

Wharton has an econometric model with 1,800

variables. It is the only service we have found that forecasts 25 years into the future. Services include

1. *Quarterly model for one year's forecast ($3,500).*
2. *Agricultural model.*
3. *World model of 35 countries that solves simultaneously for all.*
4. *Annual industrial model (the one that forecasts 25 years out) costs $9,500 per year with time sharing, $6,500 per year without.*

INTERNATIONAL

BUSINESS INTERNATIONAL
1 Dag Hammarskjold Plaza
New York, New York 10017   (212) 750-6300

These people publish seven weekly publications:

1. *Business Eastern Europe, $528 per year*
2. *Business Asia, $390 per year*
3. *Business Latin America, $395 per year*
4. *Business International, $395 per year*
5. *Business China, $215 per year*
6. *Business Europe, $648 per year*
7. *International Money Report, $565 per year*

These publications are eight-page synopses of business activity in the international field. Highly recommended as a quick and easy way of knowing the various economies. In *Business Europe,* an economic outlook for one specific country appears weekly.

Business International has a huge library filled with reports on businesses, industries, economies, resources, labor availability, and so on that is open to clients by appointment and by special permission to nonclients. If they don't have the specific report, they have the manpower to put together a report on any market in the world for a fee. Use them. A good resource for the money.

FOOD AND AGRICULTURAL ORGANIZATION OF
THE UNITED NATIONS (FAO)
Economic and Social Department of FAO
Assistant Director-General E.M. Ojala
Via Delle Terne di Caràcalla, Rome, Italy

Primarily agricultural forecasting. If it has done a study, it will let you know. Publications are available through the United Nations' publications in New York. If you write to Italy, you should receive a reasonably quick response.

INTERNATIONAL BANK FOR
RECONSTRUCTION AND DEVELOPMENT
(WORLD BANK)
1818 H Street, N.W.
Washington, D.C. 20433

The World Bank will open its library to anyone. Good statistics on foreign countries are available there.

WORLD RESOURCES INVENTORY
2500 Market Street
Philadelphia, Pennsylvania 19104

Projects to the year 2000 technical, social, environmental, and resources changes. It is an inventory, so you provide your own analysis.
See, also, under *The Economy:*

Brookings Institution,
Chase Econometrics,
Data Resources,
The Economist,
Predicasts,

195

Stanford Research Institute,
Wharton Econometrics.

Under *General:*

The Conference Board,
Daniells, Lorna,
State universities,
Governmental agencies.

Under *Technology:*

Battelle Institute,
Planned Innovation,
Technological Forecasting Techniques.

Under *The Future:*

Congressional Clearing House for the Future,
Facing the Future,
Future Research Group LOC,
The Futures Directory,
The Future File,
Futures,
Omni,
Forecasting International Ltd.,
World Future Society.

TECHNOLOGY

"Office machines that talk to each other are far different than those of 102 years ago when Alexander Graham Bell sent his voice over a wire. Upon being informed of this, the chief engineer of the British Post Office was asked: 'Do you think this machine will be of any use in Great Britain?'

He replied: 'No, sir. The Americans have need of the telephone, but we do not. We have plenty of messenger boys.' "

(*Nation's Business*, February 1979.)

BATTELLE—Institute e.V.
Am Romerhof 35
6000 Frankfurt am Main
Federal Republic of Germany
(one of the research centers of Battelle Memorial)
(0611) 79081

    or

BATTELLE MEMORIAL INSTITUTE
505 King Avenue
Columbus, Ohio 43201   (614) 424-6424

Battelle (Columbus) conducts over 3,300 studies annually in the areas of manufacturing technology, health, energy, food and agriculture, the environment, and community life. It maintains a library of 150,000 volumes. A list of published papers and articles is available.

EXECUCOM
Post Office Box 9758
Austin, Texas

Execucom Systems Corporation is a Texas-based planning and consulting firm. It offers seminars on increasing planning and decision-making effectiveness with the use of computers.

THE HUDSON INSTITUTE
Quaker Ridge Road
Croton-on-Hudson, New York 10520

(914) 762-0700

Under the auspices of Herman Kahn, The Hudson Institute has become a leading think tank for the future. You should write for a list of research projects available for a fee.

LONG-RANGE PLANNING
Superintendent of Documents
U.S. Government Printing Office
Washington, D.C.

Published in 1976, *Long-Range Planning* was prepared by the Committee on Science and Technology's subcommittee on the environment and atmosphere. It contains technological forecasts for both government and private business. Very inexpensive source, but a lot of reading.

OFFICE OF TECHNOLOGY ASSESSMENT
119 D Street, N.E.
Washington, D.C. 20510   (202) 224-6019

OTA was established by Congress in 1973 to research the effects of technological innovations. Write for information.

PLANNED INNOVATION
Published by NPM Infolink Ltd.
New Product Management Group
Management House, Parker Street
London, WC2B 5 PT, United Kingdom

'The international journal for new product management." *Planned Innovation* is a good journal for medium-sized companies. It has articles and abstracts on product planning, technology transfer, manufacturing opportunities, patent and trademarks, product design, corporate communication, and franchising and market representation. For $124 per year, you can find out where the British are coming from—or going to. An absolute wealth of information on new technologies and conferences and books dealing with technology.

TECHNOLOGICAL FORECASTING TECHNIQUES
by Erick Jantsch
Published by Organization for Economic Cooperation and Development (OECD) 1967
2, rue André-Pascal
Paris, France

This book is 12 years old, but it remains the most comprehensive and accurate book on forecasting technology. If you don't want to go to France to get it, you might be able to order it through OECD, 1750 Pennsylvania Avenue, Washington, D.C.

THE FUTURE

Forecasting in the 1980s will not be like forecasting in the 70s.

Lorna Daniells

APPLIED FUTURES, INC.
William W. Simmons, President
22 Greenwich Plaza
Greenwich, Connecticut 06830   (203) 661-9711

This private consulting/marketing firm applies the Delphi technique to planning processes via the "CON-SENSOR" (a tool). Publications include:

"A Strategic Planning Program for the Next Decade"
(American Management Journal, *January 1975);*
"What the Future Holds for Today's Managers"
(Managers' Forum, *Vol. 2, No. 1, January 1975).*

THE COMMITTEE FOR THE FUTURE, INC.
2325 Porter Street, N.W.
Washington, D.C. 20008   (202) 966-8776

The Committee for the Future forecasts beyond the year 2000 in the holistic, social, technological, environmental, resources, and educational fields. It is a small nonprofit organization.

CONGRESSIONAL CLEARING HOUSE
FOR THE FUTURE
1722 House Annex No. 1
Washington, D.C.   (202) 224-3121

This friendly group formed by Congress has a monthly publication called *What's Next,* which describes and assesses technological innovation. It lists legislation, press items, and the content of congressional debates on long-range trends, forecasts, alternatives and innovations, as printed in the *Congressional Record. What's Next* also publishes a calendar of weekly seminars held by the Committee on the Future with a *detailed* bibliography of articles and books used in the seminars.

FACING THE FUTURE:
MASTERING THE PROBABLE AND
MANAGING THE UNPREDICTABLE
Published by OECD
1750 Pennsylvania Avenue
Washington, D.C.   (202) 729-1857

The "Interfutures Group" was a special committee of the OECD that set out to study advancing industries and the development of society. Its study culminated in this book, which was published in December 1978 and is available for $22.75 (postpaid) from the above address.

"THE FUTURE"
(article in *Business Week,* September 3, 1979, pp. 167–212)

"The Future" discusses probable changes in U.S. business over the next 50 years. "People will live better, but futurists doubt they'll be much happier."

THE FUTURES RESEARCH GROUP
The Congressional Research Service
The Library of Congress
Washington, D.C. 20540   (202) 426-6498

These librarians have been working to compile a "Futures Information Retrieval System (FIRST)," which includes bibliographies, information, trends, forecasts, directory-type data, interactive programs/models.

The group has innumerable publications. Write for their lists. You can probably obtain them free from your congressperson.

THE FUTURES DIRECTORY
Compiled by John McHale and Magda Cordell Hale
IPC Science and Technology Press Ltd. (1977)
IPC HOUSE
32 High Street
Guildford, Surrey
England GU1 3EW

"An international listing and description of organizations and individuals active in future studies and long-range planning." More information than you'll ever want, but neatly arranged for easy use.

THE FUTURE FILE
By Paul Dixon
Published by Avon Books, a division of the Hearst Corporation
959 Eighth Avenue
New York, New York

For $1.95 you can have a paperback that speculates on the best and the worst possible forecasts of the future. It includes a list of organizations for the future, a glossary of futuristic terms and a delightful collection of past predictions—the worst ones ever made.

THE FUTURE GROUP, INC.
Theodore J. Gordon, President
124 Hebron Avenue
Glastonbury, Connecticut 06033   (203) 633-3501

The Future Group is one of the best think tanks. It does reports for private enterprise as well as for the government. Hard copies of in-depth studies of government and industry relations, the U.S. economy, livestock, and legalized gambling (to name a few) are available for a price. Write to see what is available and for what price. This is a first-class outfit.

FUTURES
Published by IPC Science and Technology Press Ltd.
IPC House
32 High Street
Guildford, Surrey
England GU1 3EW

A bimonthly scholarly journal that publishes *semi*-technical articles and news dealing with the future at a cost of $65.00 per year.

OMNI
Omni Publications International Ltd.
909 Third Avenue
New York, New York 10022

"*Omni* gets you thinking about the future." It is a monthly magazine that is part science fiction, part avant garde thinking about technology, medicine and so on. The cover is always intriguing. A bargain at $18.00 per year.

FORECASTING INTERNATIONAL, LTD.
1001 North Highland Street
Arlington, Virginia 22201   (703) 527-1311

Forecasting is considered to be one of the two or three outstanding private research groups in the United States. Works for private enterprise, will research anything.

WORLD FUTURE SOCIETY
4916 St. Elmo Avenue
Washington, D.C. 20014   (301) 656-8274

World Future Society forecasts 5 to 50 years into the future. A sure bet for interesting information. It has chapters or coordinators in 91 cities all over the world. Not only does it publish the journals listed below, but it also has organized special studies in sections on business, communications, education, food, government, habitats, health, human values, international affairs, life-styles, population, resources, technology, and work and careers. Its publications include *The Future: A Guide to Information Sources,* a book that holds the all-time record for being the most comprehensive collection of organizations, people, books, periodicals, media, games, research projects, and courses on the future. Published in 1977 with a revised edition in 1979, 554 pages, neatly arranged; the 1977 edition costs $17.50.

World Future Society journals include

1. Business Tomorrow, *semiannual publication, $9.00 per year for nonmembers.*
2. The Futurist, *bimonthly, $15.00 per year. (This one not only forecasts but makes suggestions as to how one might improve the future!)*

3. Careers Tomorrow, *bimonthly, $9.00 per year.*
4. Communications Tomorrow, *bimonthly, $9.00 per year.*
5. Food Tomorrow, *bimonthly, $9.00 per year.*
6. Government Tomorrow, *bimonthly, $9.00 per year.*
7. Habitats Tomorrow, *bimonthly, $9.00 per year.*
8. Health Tomorrow, *bimonthly, $9.00 per year.*
9. Human Values Tomorrow, *bimonthly, $9.00 per year.*
10. International Affairs Tomorrow, *bimonthly, $9.00 per year.*
11. Resources Tomorrow, *bimonthly, $9.00 per year.*
12. Technology Tomorrow, *bimonthly, $9.00 per year.*
13. Future Survey, *new monthly journal that can help you choose your best options for the future. It abstracts articles from books and journals relating to forecasts, trends, and ideas about the future. $36.00 for nonmembers.*

CODA: WHEN ALL ELSE FAILS

Forget all that library work, hang up the phone, throw away your regression analysis. If you can live with very short-term forecasting, here are two free indicators of economic activity one year hence as reflected in the stock market.

The Boston Snow Index (BSI). If there is snow on the ground in Boston on Christmas Day, stock prices will be up the next year. Seventy-three percent accurate since 1960. Invented by David L. Upshaw, vice president in the research department of Drexel Burnham Lambert, Inc.

The Super Bowl Indicator, discovered by Leonard Koppett, sportswriter, Palo Alto, California. If a former NFL team wins the Super Bowl in January, the stock market will be up the following December. (If you ever want to give a bookie a stock market tip.)

(Both indexes were reported in *The Wall Street Journal* Aug. 27, 1979.)

EIGHT

Author Information

Ratty-looking bunch, but they
work cheap.

DICK LEVIN, Author. Associate Dean and Professor of Business Administration, School of Business Administration, University of North Carolina at Chapel Hill. Teacher of business policy and new venture management in the MBA program. Has turned a dollar as an engineer, piano player, bandleader, Air Force officer, teacher, writer, consultant, and real estate investor. Likes the limelight—most recent stage appearance in Chapel Hill was in the dramatic parody *Yiddlers on the Spoof* as the Magic Fairy in pink wings, white tutu, purple tights. Flies his Twin-Comanche when the sky is blue.

JOHN BRANCH, Cartoonist. University of North Carolina graduate, Chapel Hill native, former editorial cartoonist for the *UNC Daily Tarheel* and *The Chapel Hill Newspaper*. Latest book of collected work entitled *Would You Buy a Used Cartoon from This Man?* Recently finished a 1–9 season with his Recreation League softball team. Had fun anyway.

GINGER TRAVIS, Editor. MBA, University of North Carolina; AB, English, Duke University. Chapel Hill resident, real estate researcher and business writer. Plays the dulcimer—knows a few old–time fiddle tunes.

INDEX

211

Index

213

Index